Incarnation and Sacrament

Incarnation and Sacrifice

Incarnation and Sacrament

The Eucharistic Controversy between Charles Hodge and John Williamson Nevin

JONATHAN G. BONOMO

WIPF & STOCK · Eugene, Oregon

INCARNATION AND SACRAMENT
The Eucharistic Controversy between Charles Hodge and John
Williamson Nevin

Wipf & Stock
An Imprint of Wipf and Stock Publishers
199 W. 8th Ave., Suite 3
Eugene, OR 97401
www.wipfandstock.com

ISBN 13: 978-1-4982-5575-2

Manufactured in the U.S.A.

For my mom and dad,
Elizabeth Bonomo and Jonathan G. Bonomo, Sr.

Contents

Foreword

THE LORD's Supper has long been a source of discussion in the Christian Church. From the ninth-century debate between Radbertus and Ratramnus, to Reformation era debates between Protestants and Catholics and between Protestants and Protestants, to contemporary debates between credo-communionists and paedo-communionists, this sacrament of union and communion has (ironically and sadly) become a point of severe disagreement.

When John Calvin came on the public scene in the 1530s, the Reformation era debates over the Lord's Supper had already been going on for years. Rome's doctrine of the Eucharistic presence and her doctrine of the Eucharistic sacrifice had both been rejected by all Protestants. They rejected Rome's doctrine of transubstantiation, and they rejected Rome's claim that the Supper was a propitiatory sacrifice. However, although they were in agreement in their rejection of Rome's doctrine, they were not able to come to agreement on the true nature of the Lord's Supper.

The Swiss Reformer Ulrich Zwingli argued that the Lord's Supper is a symbolic memorial, an initiatory ceremony in which the believer pledges that he is a Christian and proclaims that he has been reconciled to God through Christ's shed blood. He believed that Christ's words: "This is my body" should be understood to mean: "This signifies my body." Martin Luther, on the other hand, believed that

Christ's words must be understood in their literal sense. He argued that although Rome's explanation of Christ's real presence in the bread and wine was wrong, the fact of Christ's real presence in the bread and wine was correct.

Zwingli had argued that the only mode of presence proper to the human body of Christ was "local presence" (the way in which physical, finite things are present in a circumscribed place). Luther disagreed and claimed that Christ's body could also be present in an "illocal" manner. According to medieval scholastic theologians, "illocal presence" referred to the way in which finite spiritual beings such as souls or angels could be present. Luther claimed that Christ's body could be present in such a manner. Luther also claimed that there is a "sacramental union" between the substance of Christ's body and the bread resulting in a new and unique substance that Luther refers to as *fleischbrot* ("flesh-bread"). Thus, according to Luther, Christ's body is supernaturally present in the Eucharist in a real and illocal manner.

Calvin's doctrine of the Lord's Supper shared some similarities with both the Zwinglian and Lutheran views, but in many ways, Calvin broke new ground in his attempt (futile as it turned out to be) to bring the Protestants together on the issue. Calvin followed Augustine in defining a sacrament as "a visible sign of a sacred thing." According to Calvin, the sacraments seal the promises found in the Word. The sacrament of the Lord's Supper specifically seals the promise that those who partake of the bread and wine in faith truly partake of the body and blood of Christ.

Calvin argued that the signs and things signified by the signs must be distinguished but not separated. The sacramental signs, therefore, are not merely symbols (as Zwingli argued), but neither are the signs transformed into the things they signify (as Rome argued) or combined in some way with the things they signify (as Luther argued). Calvin repeatedly stressed that his disagreement with the Roman Catholics and with Luther was not over the fact of Christ's presence, but only over the mode of that presence. With Zwingli, Calvin argued that Christ's human body is locally present in heaven, but he also argued (contra Zwingli) that Christ's body does not have to be locally present on earth in order for believers to partake of it because the Holy Spirit effects our union and communion with him. Thus, what the minister does on the earthly plane with the sacramental signs, the Holy Spirit does on a parallel spiritual plane with the things signified. Those who partake of the bread and wine in faith are by the power of the Holy Spirit being nourished by the body and blood of Christ. Exactly how this is accomplished, Calvin admits, is a profound mystery.

During the sixteenth century, many of the first Reformed theologians and confessions adopted Calvin's doctrine of the Lord's Supper. However, over time, some Reformed theologians moved away from Calvin's doctrine toward a more Zwinglian doctrine. By the time of the nineteenth century, Calvin's doctrine of the Supper was the minority view among Reformed Christians. This gradual move away from Calvin's doctrine went unnoticed by some and was encouraged by others. One nineteenth-century American theologian, however, was not pleased with the development, and his book arguing for a return to Calvin's view sparked one of the most interesting debates in American Church history.

John Williamson Nevin was something of an anomaly
in the nineteenth-century American church. In the midst
of a church that had been heavily influenced by the new
measures revivalism of Charles Finney, anti-clerical and
primitivist restorationism, democratic individualism,
Baconianism and Scottish common-sense realism stood
this confessional Calvinist with high views of the church,
the creeds, and the sacraments. In 1846, Nevin published
*The Mystical Presence: A Vindication of the Reformed or
Calvinistic Doctrine of the Holy Eucharist*. This work was
an impassioned plea to return to the doctrine of the Lord's
Supper taught by Calvin and the early Reformed confessions. His book did not escape the notice of the most prominent nineteenth-century Reformed theologian in America,
Princeton Seminary's Charles Hodge. Two years after the
publication of Nevin's book, Hodge wrote a scathing review
in the *Biblical Repertory and Princeton Review*. Hodge took
Nevin to task on a number of issues in addition to his claims
about Calvin's doctrine of the Lord's Supper. Nevin did not
hesitate to defend himself.

The debate between Nevin and Hodge is instructive,
not only for what it teaches us about each man's view of
the Lord's Supper, but also for what it reveals about their
(and our) underlying theological and philosophical presuppositions. The value of studying their debate has become
more evident in recent years and has begun to attract more
and more scholarly attention. Within the last several years
a number of monographs and articles dealing with one
aspect or another of the debate have appeared. The work
you hold in your hands by Jonathan Bonomo is a valuable
contribution to the ongoing scholarly discussion. Bonomo

carefully digs beneath the surface of the debate, revealing the important underlying differences that made it difficult for Nevin and Hodge to understand each other and virtually impossible for them to agree. For those interested in the Nevin/Hodge debate specifically or nineteenth-century American Christianity generally, it should become required reading.

Keith A. Mathison
Ligonier Academy
Orlando, Florida

Preface

THIS BOOK is a revised and updated version of the Master's thesis I wrote as a Church history student at Gordon-Conwell Theological Seminary, in 2008. It has as its subject a theological controversy which took place between two Reformed theologians in the United States during the middle of the nineteenth century on the doctrine of the Eucharist. As such, it is most immediately a study in American religious and intellectual history.

But the Eucharistic controversy between Charles Hodge and John Williamson Nevin is more than a purely academic exercise. Hodge and Nevin battled over issues that lie at the heart of Christian faith and piety—issues which have been a bone of contention in the universal Church for many, many centuries, such as: Why, exactly, did God become man? What bearing does the incarnation of Christ have on the redemption of the world? What is the relation between the divine and human natures in the one person of Jesus Christ? How are believers on earth truly united with the ascended Christ in heaven? Is Christ really present in the Lord's Supper? If so, then how is he made to be present? These are questions that most thoughtful Christians in every age of the Church have asked at one point or another. And it was these age-old questions that Charles Hodge and John W. Nevin sought to answer, and over which they came to vigorously contend.

Literature on the Mercersburg Theology has been on the rise in recent years. W. Bradford Littlejohn's excellent work, *The Mercersburg Theology and the Quest for Reformed Catholicity*, published in 2009, is one example of particular worth to which the current volume may prove complimentary, although this was not my original intention. I came to read Littlejohn's book shortly after Wipf and Stock had offered to publish my own thesis, and I was soon impressed by how similar our respective takes on the Mercersburg Theology are. Nevertheless, I trust that the publication of this present work is not a superfluous undertaking. While a good deal of the current literature on Mercersburg has a rather broad scope, this book offers a focused look at one episode in particular. It provides an analysis and assessment of the historical, philosophical, and theological aspects of the Eucharistic controversy between Charles Hodge and John W. Nevin, specifically. The interaction between these two nineteenth century Reformed theologians will, I hope, shed some light on the backgrounds of the sacramental theology (or lack thereof) held by American Christians of the general Reformed persuasion in the twenty-first century. As both Hodge and Nevin were two of the most important thinkers in the history of the American Church, we would do well to listen to their various insights and concerns on these vital matters.

I am regrettably persuaded, as John Nevin was in his own day, that American Protestants in general suffer from historical amnesia. We have a tendency to act in the present without considering the past, because we generally think of ourselves (even if we wouldn't put it in quite these terms) as those who have finally arrived at the point of having figured it all out on our own. But we do not exist in a historical vacuum. We are greatly indebted to the insights and successes of those who have gone before us, and we have also been shaped by their faults and failures. We therefore neglect our past at our own peril.

Thus, it is my desire that this book would help to provide some illumination on the theological heritage of the Protestant churches in the United States, and in particular the Protestant churches of the Reformed tradition in the United States. The two great nineteenth century theologians who are the subject of this volume provide a mirror, so to speak, in which we might see a reflection of our own ecclesial faces. By looking attentively into their various idiosyncrasies and differences, we may attain greater understanding of who we are as a Church collectively, and also of who we are as particular churches which continue to be separated by many of the same issues Nevin and Hodge argued about a century and a half ago.

There are quite a few individuals who deserve thanks for their help along the way as I researched, pondered, wrote, and re-wrote this book—to be sure, many more than I have opportunity to acknowledge here. But the following people are those who have had their hands most immediately in whatever virtues it may have, though they are not in any way responsible for its remaining deficiencies. The encouragement and guidance of Gordon-Conwell professors Richard Lints, Gwenfair Walters Adams, and Garth M. Rossell was instrumental throughout the initial stages of my research on the thought of John W. Nevin and Philip Schaff, while John Jefferson Davis offered helpful comments during my thesis defense, and encouraged some important revisions. Further, I wish to thank Dr. Gordon L. Isaac, my thesis advisor, for his initial encouragement to pursue my interest in the Eucharistic controversy between Nevin and Hodge specifically, and for the helpful direction he provided throughout the process of research and writing. The perspective gained during our various conversations while I was working through the issues between Nevin and Hodge was invaluable. In addition, thanks must go to Keith A. Mathison of Ligonier Academy, for reading the original thesis and encouraging me to pursue publication, as well as for his continued help along the way. And I would be remiss if I neglected to also mention the wonderful congregation of Calvary Presbyterian Church in Willow Grove, Pennsylvania—in particular pastors Richard Tyson and Gregg MacDougall—for their constant support, encouragement, and guidance. They have made the presence and love of Jesus Christ tangible to me week in and week out, thus ensuring that my undertaking of a work such as this would not merely be an exercise in intellectual abstraction. Finally, and most importantly, it is a joy to have the opportunity to thank my dear wife, Yvonne. As anyone well acquainted with us already knows, my every endeavor would be utterly hopeless without her wisdom, devotion, and support. This book is no exception.

Jonathan G. Bonomo, Jr.
Glenside, Pennsylvania
January 21, 2010

Introduction

THE NINETEENTH century was a period of dramatic theological development and change. The Reformation of the sixteenth century had given rise to various Protestant theological traditions that, with the passing of centuries, were developing, solidifying, and in some cases splintering. The philosophical movements that came to dominate the thought patterns of the modern world such as Enlightenment rationalism, German idealism, and Scottish Common Sense realism made their way into the life of the Christian church, thereby facilitating the development of corresponding theological systems. Examples of this may be seen in a wide range of movements, such as Friedrich Schleiermacher's theological system and the later mediating theology in Germany, the Oxford Movement in England, and the revitalization of Reformed scholasticism in Scotland and America.

One affect of this changing theological scene on the ecclesiastical shape of nineteenth century America was that it encouraged the establishment of competing theological schools and seminaries throughout the country. Consequently, as E. Brooks Holifield has noted, "as theology moved from the parishes to the seminaries, rivalries among the schools intensified theological disagreements."[1] Two of the most important among these competing seminaries by

1. Holifield, *Theology in America*, 371.

the middle of the nineteenth century were Princeton, the Presbyterian seminary in New Jersey, and Mercersburg, the German Reformed seminary in Pennsylvania. [2]

Charles Hodge (1797–1878) and John Williamson Nevin (1803–86) are the two theologians who are most representative of the theology produced at these two institutions (Hodge at Princeton and Nevin at Mercersburg). They were among the most brilliant theological lights to labor in the United States in the nineteenth century. Both were born on American soil, both were reared in old school Presbyterian homes, and both were heirs and advocates of the Reformed tradition. Nevertheless, as their thought developed, they came to differ dramatically in a number of important ways, not the least of these being the topics of Christology, soteriology, and their understanding of the nature and significance of the Church and the sacraments. And beneath all of their particular differences there existed between Hodge and Nevin a fundamental variance at the level of foundational philosophical principles and overall theological method.

The most interesting and revealing of the numerous theological conflicts that took place between these two theologians was occasioned by a literary debate over the

2. Princeton was by far more important than Mercersburg in the nineteenth century with regard to its influence in terms of numbers as well as the respect it garnered from various quarters. However, Mercersburg must also be considered one of the most important theological schools of the nineteenth century because of the unique and profound theological system that was produced there by John Nevin, along with his Swiss-born colleague, Philip Schaff. Through their works, the theology of Mercersburg continues to captivate and instruct the thinking of many theological students to the present day.

doctrine of the Reformed Church on the Lord's Supper. This particular controversy began with the publication in 1846 of John W. Nevin's masterful historical-theological work on the Eucharist, entitled *The Mystical Presence: A Vindication of the Reformed or Calvinistic Doctrine of the Holy Eucharist*. And the debate continued as an ongoing literary conflict throughout subsequent years in a variety of publications.

It is the purpose of the present work to offer a historical and theological analysis and assessment of this controversy. In the process, I hope to demonstrate how the diverging theological presuppositions held by these two great Reformed theologians dramatically affected their respective theological systems and led them toward differing conceptions of the person and work of Jesus Christ, his relation to the world in general and his people in particular, the Church and the sacraments, and even the nature of Christianity itself.

Chapter one sets the stage of the controversy by offering an overview of the central tenets of the Princeton Theology of Charles Hodge and the Mercersburg Theology of John Williamson Nevin. This charting out of the general theological trajectories of these two divergent theological systems will provide the historical-theological context for the controversy with which we are primarily concerned.

Chapter two consists of a close analysis of the Eucharistic controversy proper. Beginning with Nevin's *Mystical Presence*, followed by Hodge's critique of this work, and concluding with Nevin's rebuttal of Hodge, we will look at the particular historical and theological arguments provided by Nevin and Hodge in support of their different interpretations of the Reformed doctrine of the Lord's Supper.

The third chapter seeks to show how the different conceptions of Hodge and Nevin on the person and work of Christ conditioned the place which the doctrine of the Eucharist held in their respective understandings of the Christian faith. To do this we go back through Nevin's *Mystical Presence*, Hodge's review, and Nevin's response, narrowing the lens this time around on their Christology, specifically.

The fourth and final chapter provides a general evaluation of the controversy in its overarching historical, philosophical, and theological contours. Pulling the lens back, we will revisit the overall theological systems of Princeton and Mercersburg in light of the Eucharistic controversy. After this, some concluding remarks about the controversy as a whole and its importance will be offered.

1

On a Collision Course—
Princeton and Mercersburg

CHARLES HODGE
AND THE PRINCETON THEOLOGY

Princeton Seminary was founded in 1812. Through the labors of such men as Archibald Alexander, Samuel Miller, and Charles Hodge, Princeton very quickly became one of the most popular theological schools in the country, and was without question the center of American Presbyterian orthodoxy throughout the nineteenth century.[1] The main figure to emerge as the Princeton mainstay was Charles Hodge, who taught there for over fifty years. During Hodge's career at Princeton—which began in 1820 as Professor of Oriental Languages and Biblical Literature—his name was virtually inseparable from the seminary. As David Wells puts it, "Princeton Theology in the early years was really Charles Hodge's theology."[2]

---

1. According to Sidney Ahlstrom: "Especially as developed and defended by Charles Hodge, the Princeton Theology became the criterion of Reformed Orthodoxy in America" (Ahlstrom, *Religious History of the American People*, 463).

2. Wells, *Reformed Theology in America*, 36.

Hodge's thought was conditioned by three things in particular: 1. a supreme regard for the Bible as the divinely inspired source of Christian doctrine, 2. the confessional Reformed tradition, primarily as articulated by the seventeenth century Reformed scholastics (above all, Francis Turretin) and the Westminster Standards, and 3. Scottish Common Sense realism, which provided the philosophical foundation for a proper understanding of the Bible as a system of doctrine.[3] These three elements were combined

3. Common Sense realism was formulated and expounded most fully in Scotland by Thomas Reid (1710–96) at Aberdeen and Glasgow and Dugald Stewart (1753–1828) at Edinburgh. This Scottish philosophy gained a wide hearing in America through the influence of John Witherspoon (1723–94) at Princeton. Witherspoon laid the philosophical foundations for what would later become the distinctive Princeton theology of Archibald Alexander and Charles Hodge as well as their successors A.A. Hodge (son of Charles) and B.B. Warfield. Due to the influence of Witherspoon, Common Sense realism had become the major philosophical underpinning of every major theological seminary in the country by the 1790s. (See Holifield, *Theology in America*, 175.)

For an excellent treatment of the influence of Scottish Common Sense philosophy on Hodge's thought, see Sydney Ahlstrom's article, "The Scottish Philosophy and American Theology." Ahlstrom points out that the Common Sense realism of Reid and Stewart is characterized by four main tenets: 1. Philosophy depends on the scientific observation of one's self-consciousness. 2. This observation establishes a set of principles, both necessary and contingent. 3. Only an intelligent being can be an efficient cause of anything. 4. "The first principles of morals are self-evident intuitions" (261). Concerning the fourth tenet listed by Ahlstrom, Claude Welch has noted that Charles Hodge "owed much to the Scottish realists, notably in his understanding of 'first truths' or 'laws of belief' that God had implanted in man's nature" (Welch, *Protestant Thought in the Nineteenth Century: vol. 1*, 202). Linden J. DeBie is also helpful in charting out the influence of Scottish realism on the thinkers at

in Hodge's brilliant mind to create one of the most lasting theological contributions of nineteenth century America.[4]

Hodge's theological purpose, therefore, was to systematize the divinely inspired facts of Scripture in an attempt to articulate what he saw as the biblical and historic Reformed faith, utilizing a scientific methodology consistent with Common Sense realism. Nowhere is this stated more clearly than in his articulation of a proper theological method found in the introduction to his *Systematic Theology*.[5] Throughout this introduction, Hodge explains that the Bible is a plain book inspired by God containing facts and doctrines to be interpreted by common reason, and that theology is the science of collecting these facts and putting them into a coherent system: "The Bible is to the theologian what nature is to the man of science. It is his store-house of facts; and his method of ascertaining what the Bible teaches, is the same as that which the natural philosopher adopts to ascertain what nature teaches."[6] Hodge goes on to further elaborate on the task of the theologian:

Princeton. See his *Speculative Theology and Common-Sense Religion*, 1–30.

4. This three-tiered authority structure has been suggested by Mark Noll, who states in his introduction to Hodge's *The Way of Life*: "For Charles Hodge, commitments to the Bible as ultimate authority, to Reformed Confessionalism as the best expression of Christian faith, and to Scottish Common Sense Realism as a philosophical guide were always part and parcel of unswerving commitment to lively religious experience" (28). The supremacy and attempted synthesis of these three authorities makes its way into the vast majority of Hodge's writings. (See Holifield, *Theology in America*, 379–81.)

5. *Systematic Theology, vol. 1*, 1–188.

6. Ibid., 10.

> [T]he duty of the Christian theologian is to as-
> certain, collect, and combine all the facts which
> God has revealed concerning himself and our
> relation to Him. These facts are all in the Bible.
> This is true, because everything revealed in na-
> ture, and in the constitution of man concerning
> God and our relation to Him, is contained and
> authenticated in Scripture. It is in this sense that
> "the Bible, and the Bible alone, is the religion of
> Protestants."[7]

This understanding of Scripture as a "store-house of facts" led Hodge to the conclusion that Christianity is fundamentally a system of doctrine: "The Apostles propounded a certain system of doctrines; they pronounced those to be Christians who received these doctrines so as to determine their character and life."[8] This is not to deny that Christianity is heavenly in nature or that it finds expression in the experience of individual believers, for Hodge clearly affirmed the actual existence of the realities which the biblical doctrines describe. Yet, in Hodge's thinking, heavenly realities and the propositions by which these realities are expressed are almost indistinguishable.

Thus, for Hodge, the objectivity of Christian truth is based on its propositional, factual character. Christianity is primarily the coherent system of doctrine reasonably deduced from the store-house of divinely revealed facts given to man by God—the Bible. To be sure, this system of doctrine must take root in the lives of people in the world,[9]

7. Ibid., 11.

8. Ibid., 177.

9. For instance, in "What is Christianity," Hodge distinguishes

but Christianity is for Charles Hodge, at bottom, a system of objective doctrinal facts.[10]

Hodge accordingly detested all forms of theological speculation, no matter how Christian or pious it might sound. For instance, in the midst of a discussion of the German mediating theology of his day (with which he equated the theology of John Williamson Nevin), he stated:

> As Christian theology is simply the exhibition and illustration of the facts and truths of the Bible in their due relations and proportions, it has nothing to do with these speculations. The "mediating theology" does not pretend to be founded on the Bible. It does not, at least in Germany, profess allegiance to the Church doctrine. It avowedly gives up Christianity as a doctrine to save it as a life. It is founded upon "speculation" and not upon authority, whether of the Scriptures or of the Church.[11]

---

between Christianity objectively considered and Christianity subjectively considered: "Christianity objectively considered, is the testimony of God concerning his Son . . . Subjectively considered, it is the life of Christ in the soul, or, that form of life which has its origin in Christ, is determined by the revelation concerning his person and work, and which is due to the indwelling of his Spirit" (119).

10. According to William DiPuccio: "Nineteenth-century Presbyterian theologians often identified the object of faith with the *propositions* of Scripture rather than with Christ Himself. Charles Hodge and others equated the objective side of Christianity with biblical propositions. Like Locke, Common Sense theology viewed revelation as essentially cognitive. Faith consists in believing *that* something is true, rather than being the means by which we participate in the realities to which such doctrines point (DiPuccio, *The Interior Sense of Scripture*, 13).

11. Hodge, *Systematic Theology, vol. 2*, 453.

These principles led Hodge to an overtly federalist theological system which thrived on the drawing of strict distinctions between the earthly and the heavenly. Hodge was therefore continually very careful to distinguish sharply between soul and body in man, sign and reality in the sacraments, and divine and human in Christ. He thus stressed above all else the distinction between the Creator and the creation.[12]

Hodge therefore consistently argued for a certain form of dualism, which he held to be clearly taught in the Bible. In his article *What is Christianity?*, for instance, in objection to John Nevin's Christology, he asserts that "Dr. Nevin denies any dualism in Christ, saying that while we may separate his Divinity from his humanity as united in his person in thought, they are nevertheless one."[13] However, this ought not to be understood in the sense of a sort of quasi-Gnosticism. While he was very concerned to tenaciously maintain the ontological distinction between Creator and creation as well as between spirit and matter, Hodge consistently affirmed the inherent goodness of the material creation and of the human body.

There is also a nominalism in Hodge's thought which pervades his theology. As William Evans puts it, "Hodge's methodological orientation toward the particular and the

12. In this respect, Hodge was a faithful expositor of his church's Confession, as may be seen in *Westminster Confession of Faith*, 7.1. John W. Nevin, for his part, did not deny that there is a *distinction* between Creator and creation, but he did consider the extent to which theologians like Charles Hodge stressed the Creator/creature distinction to border on complete separation, which he saw as leading to a dualism that compromised the true meaning of the incarnation.

13. Hodge, *What is Christianity*, 145.

individual at the expense of the general lends a nominalistic caste to his theology. This was, in fact, a persistent charge leveled against Hodge by his contemporaries." [14] So, in his article *Nature of Man*, Hodge argues that, "There may be convenient formulas to prevent circumventions, and to express a class of fact. But they do not convey any definite idea beyond the facts themselves. To say that a whole forest of oaks have the same generic life, that they are as truly one as any individual tree is one, means simply that the nature is the same in all, and that all have been derived from a common source." [15] This way of thinking had dramatic implications for how Hodge conceived of the relation of mankind to Adam, and consequently also for his understanding of the significance and purpose of the incarnation, person, and work of the Son of God, as well as the relation of Christ to his people.

For Hodge, Adam was above all the representative of the race. The connection that human beings bear to him is to be located in the fact that he was, as the first particular man, ordained by God as their representative. This led Hodge to view the imputation of Adam's first sin to his posterity as immediate and legal in nature. Men are imputed with the guilt of Adam's sin by divine fiat, and their subsequent corruption is the consequence of this divine decree.

Accordingly therefore, in redemption the eternal Logos became a man primarily so that he could be the representative of those who would be united to him by faith. In his office as the second representative man, Christ lived a perfectly righteous life and died for his people in their

14. Evans, *Imputation and Impartation*, 330.
15. Hodge, "Nature of Man," 124.

room and stead. And those who believe this gospel are judicially declared to be righteous on the basis of the divine decree to impute Christ's righteousness to them.

There is consequently very little emphasis on any inward or organic connection in Hodge's system, whether between Adam and the race or between Christ and his people. The relation is strictly forensic:

> Adam was the head and representative of his race. We stood our probation in him. His sin was putatively the sin of his posterity. It was the judicial ground of their condemnation. The penalty of that transgression was death, the loss of the life of God, as well as his fellowship and favour. All mankind, therefore, represented by Adam in the first covenant, came into the world in a state of condemnation and of spiritual death. He was a type of Christ, because Christ is the head and representative of His people. He fulfilled all righteousness in their behalf and in their stead. As Adam's disobedience was the ground of the condemnation of all who were in him, so Christ's obedience is the ground for the justification of all who are in Him; and as spiritual death was the penal, and therefore certain consequence of our condemnation for the sin of Adam, so spiritual and eternal life is the covenanted, and therefore the certain and inseparable consequence of our justification for the righteousness of Christ.[16]

16. Hodge, *Systematic Theology, vol. 2,* 538.

Hodge believed this representative principle to be so vital in fact that he claimed that it is "fundamental to the Protestant theology."[17]

This systematic, distinction oriented theological method of Hodge brought him up against all theologians who opted for a more speculative and mystical conception of the Christian faith. One of the most notable and able of Hodge's opponents in this regard was a brilliant Reformed theologian himself, who had been educated under Hodge at Princeton—John Williamson Nevin.

JOHN WILLIAMSON NEVIN AND THE MERCERSBURG THEOLOGY

After graduating from Princeton, John W. Nevin was actually appointed by Charles Hodge to fill in for him for two years teaching Hebrew while Hodge studied in Germany.[18] He eventually took a position as chair of Biblical Literature at the newly founded Western Theological Seminary in Pittsburgh, where he immersed himself in the thought of the sixteenth century Reformers as well as the early Church Fathers. From Pittsburgh Nevin accepted a call in 1840 to become Professor of Theology at the German Reformed Church's seminary in Mercersburg, Pennsylvania.

17. Hodge, "The First and the Second Adam," 341.

18. It is hard not to be struck by the irony of this arrangement. The one American theologian whose theology Hodge would come to continually assault for being far too influenced by German speculative theologians is here appointed by Hodge to take over his teaching responsibilities while Hodge goes to Germany in order to study under those very speculative theologians!

The situation in which Nevin found himself at Mercersburg left much to be desired. Scott Francis Brenner has described the state of the seminary upon his arrival well: "Nevin found himself head of a Seminary that had no money, no professors, and a student body that always reminded him of the collect 'where two or three are gathered. '"[19] Within a short period of time, however, Nevin would revitalize the seminary and in many ways the entire denomination. With the arrival of Philip Schaff in 1844, the two great historical theologians would collaborate as the chief formulators of one of the most original and fascinating theological systems of nineteenth century America.[20] It was during his career at Mercersburg, which was just over a decade long, that Nevin would produce the majority of his best known and most representative theological works. In the writings penned throughout his years at the seminary, he articulated the main tenets of what came to be known as the Mercersburg Theology.

Nevin was an altogether different sort of theologian than Charles Hodge. He drank deeply from the tradition of the Church through history, both before and after the Reformation, and he was also thoroughly influenced by nineteenth century German idealist philosophy. These influ-

19. Brenner, "Nevin and the Mercersburg Theology," 50–51.

20. Brenner notes the significance of the combination of Nevin and Schaff at Mercersburg: "The meeting of Nevin and Schaff was like the concurrence of two heavenly bodies of the first magnitude. The splendor which ensued is known as the Mercersburg Theology, for these two intellectual giants of the Presbyterian-Reformed household of faith wrought out a theological system of singular boldness, relevant to its time distinctively ecumenical, and of unquestioned enduring worth" (Ibid. 51).

ences brought him—in contrast to Hodge—to formulate a theological system that stressed the universal, mystical, and organic over the particular, propositional, and forensic. His theology took form as a sort of synthesis between patristic thought, Reformed Protestantism, and a modified German idealism, particularly as this philosophy is represented in the nineteenth century German mediating theologians who were Nevin's contemporaries.[21]

Nevin came to view Christianity not, like Hodge, primarily as a system of doctrines, but more fundamentally as a *life*. According to him, "Christianity is no . . . outward statute-book of things to be believed and things to be done. It is the law of life in Christ Jesus. It is a new constitution of grace and truth starting in Christ's *person*, and perpetuating itself in this form, as a most real historical fact, by the Church."[22]

21. The more conservative theological heirs of the thought of F. D. E. Schleiermacher and G. F. W. Hegel in nineteenth century Germany are commonly referred to as "mediating theologians" because their purpose was to make the theological system of Schleiermacher and the idealism of Hegel more consistent with historic, orthodox Christianity. Representative among the German mediating theologians are Carl Immanuel Nitzsch (1787–1868), Karl Ulmann (1796–1865), August D. C. Twesten (1789–1876), Alexander Schweizer (1808–88), Julius Muller (1801–79), K.H. Sack (1789–1875) and, most notably, Isaak Dorner (1809–84). For a survey of the mediating theologians and their overall project, see Welch, *Protestant Thought*, 269–82. For an excellent analysis of the influence of the mediating theologians on the Mercersburg theology, see particularly DeBie, *Speculative Theology*, 31–75. Also of note in this regard are DiPuccio's essay, "Nevin's Idealistic Philosophy," (*Reformed Confessionalism*, edited by Hamstra and Griffioen, 43–67), and Carlough, "German Idealism and the Theology of John W. Nevin."

22. Nevin, *Catholic and Reformed*, 153.

In a letter to Dr. Henry Harbaugh, Nevin provides a concise description of his theology, making it clear that the Person of Christ is the central feature of his thought: "The distinguishing character of the Mercersburg Theology, in one word, is its Christological interest, its way of looking at all things through the Person of the crucified and risen Savior."[23] This "Christological interest" focuses on three areas in particular: the incarnation of the eternal Logos, the organic union between the incarnate Christ and the human race, and the mystical union of Christ with his people.

Earlier in the same letter to Harbaugh, Nevin had declared concerning his theological system that, "Its cardinal principle is the fact of the Incarnation. This viewed not as a doctrine or speculation but as a real transaction of God in the world, is regarded as being necessarily itself the essence of Christianity, the sum and substance of the whole Christian redemption. Christ saves the world, not ultimately by what he teaches or what he does, but by what he *is* in the constitution of his own person."[24] Thus, it is the Incarnation—the union of the divine Logos with humanity in the person of Jesus Christ—that is the heart of Christianity in Nevin's system; and this not conceived simply as an isolated doctrine or proposition, but as a real, enduring, tangible fact—"a real transaction of God in the world."

This is a theme that is reiterated throughout Nevin's writings. Everything the Mercersburg system seeks to communicate has its foundation in the person of Jesus Christ. Indeed, for Nevin, the mystery of the incarnation brought

23. Ibid., 410.
24. Ibid., 408.

Christianity into existence and is therefore the standpoint from which every Christian doctrine is to be viewed:

> As an object of faith and knowledge, and in the only form in which it can be regarded as having any reality in the world, Christianity has been brought to pass through the mystery of the Incarnation, and stands perpetually in the presence and power of that fact. All its verities, all its doctrines, all its promises, all its driving forces, root themselves continually in the undying life of Him, who thus became man for us men and for our salvation.[25]

Whereas Charles Hodge's system was conditioned by a nominalist bent, Nevin's incarnation-centered theology presupposes a realist metaphysic which perceives universals as having an objective existence that lies behind and grounds the existence of particulars. So, for Nevin, generic human nature has an existence of its own that underlies the being of particular human persons.[26] Adam's fall from righteousness therefore affected all mankind because human nature, in its universal conception, has its origin in him. When Adam fell, humanity as a whole fell in him. As Nevin puts it, "The ruin in which we lie is an organic ruin; the ruin of our nature; universal and whole, not simply because all men are sinners, but as making all men to be sinners."[27]

---

25. Ibid. 365.

26. Nevin frequently raised the realist banner against the nominalist anthropology of theologians like Hodge, often claiming that such a theory turns humanity into nothing more than a great sand heap. See, for instance, "Wilberforce on the Eucharist," 177.

27. Nevin, *The Mystical Presence*, 155.

Thus, in redemption also, where the federalist Princeton theology demands that Christ be conceived primarily as *a particular man*—the one who came to Earth in order to *do* what no other human being could not do, as the representative of his people—the Mercersburg theology demands a conception of the incarnation that locates its primary significance in Christ as *the universal man*—the one who became incarnate in order to *be* what no human being could be. For Nevin, then, the incarnation of the Son of God is the fundamental fact of Christian redemption because in it God was organically united with universal humanity in the Person of Jesus:

> That the race might be saved, it was necessary that a work should be wrought not beyond it, but in it; and this inward salvation to be effective must lay hold of the race itself in its organic, universal character, before it could extend to individuals, since in no other form was it possible for it to cover fully the breadth and depth of the ruin that lay in its way. Such an inward salvation of the race required that it should be joined in a living way with the divine nature itself, as represented by the everlasting Word or *Logos*, the fountain of all created light and life. The Word accordingly became flesh, that is assumed humanity into union with itself.[28]

Flowing from this understanding of the organic union between Christ and humanity is Nevin's perspective on the believer's mystical union with Christ. According to him, the salvation of a Christian is not merely an abstract idea con-

28. Ibid. 156.

tained in a certain order of doctrines; rather, it is an existential fact of the believer's life. Jesus Christ communicates his divine-human life to his people in a real, substantial way, activating within them a heavenly power that renews their corrupted nature, eventually culminating in the eschatological resurrection.[29]

Nevin's theological system will be expounded in more detail in the subsequent chapters (as will that of Hodge). But let it simply be observed at this point that, in contrast to the dualistic trajectory of Hodge's thought, Nevin's Mercersburg Theology is fundamentally a system of union, having its foundation in the union of divine and human in the person of Jesus Christ. The hypostatic union of Christ's dual natures in the incarnation leads to his organic union with human nature in general and to his mystical union with the community of the redeemed in particular, through his death and resurrection. As David Layman puts it, "For Nevin, the incarnation is not primarily a doctrine, law, or even an event; it is an 'historical enduring fact' . . . The incarnation inserts a new realm of powers, a new spiritual reality, into the material."[30]

THE ENSUING CONFLICT

Both Charles Hodge and John Williamson Nevin claimed to be legitimate heirs of the historic Reformed tradition. Yet with theological principles that diverged so dramati-

---

29. Ibid. 166. DiPuccio puts it well when he says that this "actualization of the ideal in space and time is . . . the *fons et origo* of the Mercersburg Theology" ("Nevin's Idealistic Philosophy," 44).

30. Layman, "Nevin's Holistic Supernaturalism," 200.

cally they were bound to collide with one another in open conflict. And collide they did. As the leading figures of two prominent seminaries, the central mouth-pieces for two of the most significant theological systems to be formulated in antebellum America, and chief editors of two of the most influential theological journals in the country, Hodge and Nevin engaged in what may justly be called open theological war throughout their careers.

The most significant particular controversy between them revolved around the doctrine of the Reformed Church on the Lord's Supper. This was not merely a historical debate concerning what the Reformed churches originally believed regarding the Eucharist. Though this was the occasion of the conflict, the debate reveals much more deeply rooted differences between these two men than their historiography of Reformation sacramentology. It was a conflict that stretched across the entire field of Christian doctrine, with two opposing sets of theological first principles as the fundamental issue. Controversy was sparked with the publication of John Williamson Nevin's classic work on the historic Calvinist doctrine of the Eucharist, *The Mystical Presence*. It is to the Eucharistic doctrine of this work that we now turn.

2

Let's Get "Real"—
The Reformed Doctrine of the Eucharist

NEVIN'S MYSTICAL PRESENCE

IN 1846 John W. Nevin published his most representative
and brilliant piece of theological writing. The full title
of the work is *The Mystical Presence: A Vindication of the
Reformed or Calvinistic Doctrine of the Holy Eucharist*. This
treatise on the historic Calvinist doctrine of the Eucharist
is widely regarded as one of the greatest and most unique
theological writings to have been produced on American
soil in the nineteenth century.[1] It was never very popular
in Nevin's own day, however, primarily because it cut completely against the grain of the vast majority of the Protestant
religion of nineteenth century America. Indeed, as Mark
Noll has pointed out, the very title of the work is "indicative
of how poorly [Nevin's] ideas fit into the voluntaristic, low-
church, often antisacramental attitudes of his age."[2]

---

1. Gerrish has stated that *The Mystical Presence* "deserves to
be ranked among the classics of American theological literature"
(*Tradition in the Modern World*, 57).

2. Noll, *America's God*, 324.

Nevin's purpose in *The Mystical Presence* was three-fold. First, he attempted to provide a restatement of historic Calvinist Eucharistic theology, primarily as it was formulated by John Calvin and set down as the consensus opinion of the Reformed churches in the sixteenth century Reformed Confessions. Second, he sought to demonstrate the widespread apostasy from this doctrine into which the nineteenth century Reformed churches in America had fallen. And third, he provided the theological foundation for his understanding of the Calvinist doctrine of the Lord's Supper in his articulation of the mystical union between Christ and the Church, while offering a slight modification of it in light of his moderate idealist metaphysic.

Even beyond these three immediate concerns, however, Nevin provides us in *The Mystical Presence* with the fullest, most systematic treatment of the main tenets of the Mercersburg Theology that he ever produced. It bespeaks the high place that both the traditions of the historic Church and the Eucharist in particular held in Nevin's thought, piety, and life that the occasion for such a complete and methodical presentation of his thinking was a "vindication" of the Calvinist doctrine of the Lord's Supper. Nevin saw the Eucharist as occupying a place of first importance in Christian faith and practice.

Nevin begins his treatment of the topic by laying out his understanding of the Calvinist doctrine of the Lord's Supper. Here he contends that the Eucharist is central to the entire system of Christianity. It cannot undergo modification without a resultant modification to the entire theological system in which it rests: "The *Question of the Eucharist* is one of the most important belonging to the history of religion. It may be regarded as in some sense central to the whole Christian system. For Christianity is grounded in the living union of the believer with the person of Christ; and this great fact is emphatically concentrated in the mystery of the Lord's Supper."[3]

The Reformed churches in America, however, had deviated from the original Reformed doctrine on this issue: "An unchurchly, rationalistic tendency, has been allowed to carry the Church gradually more and more off from the ground it occupied in the beginning, till its position is found to be at length, to a large extent, a new one altogether."[4] As this is the case, and since the doctrine of the Eucharist is in some sense central to Christianity itself, it is safe to assume, according to Nevin, that the Church of the nineteenth century had fallen into an entirely new system of doctrine.

Nevin claims that the foundation of the historic Reformed doctrine is the "idea of an inward living union of believers with Christ."[5] By virtue of this union believers are "mystically inserted more and more into the person of Christ." It is above all this process of ongoing mystical union with Christ that had always been thought by the Reformed churches to be most fully realized and confirmed to believers in the Supper.[6] The union to which Nevin refers here is not merely moral or forensic, but "organic" and "mystical." This does include moral and forensic union, but in order to have any true effect in the actual lives of Christians, the union they have with Christ must go beyond that which

3. Nevin, *Mystical Presence*, 47.

4. Ibid., 48.

5. Ibid., 50.

6. Ibid., 51.

is merely formal or outward and penetrate into their very being. Similarly, in the Lord's Supper the believer does not only partake of formal symbols, nor simply of symbols accompanied by promises and a remembrance of what Christ has done on their behalf, but with the very life and substance of the Savior himself, "made present to us . . . by the power of the Holy Ghost."[7]

Thus, a true, mystical union of Christ with believers is foundational for taking part in the reality of the Eucharistic transaction. External imputation must be made internal and actually transferred into the person of the believer for any reception of the substance of Christ's body and blood to take place. Hence, Nevin is careful to reject any understanding of the Sacrament that would imply a *manducatio impiorum.*[8] Nevertheless, the presence of Christ in the sacrament is not on this account any less real. According to Nevin, as a real transaction brought to pass by the operation of the Holy Spirit, the presence of Christ in the Supper is:

7. Ibid., 53.

8. Ibid., 55. *Manducatio impiorum* ("eating of the ungodly") was a key phrase at issue between the Lutheran and Reformed parties in the Eucharistic controversies which took place among Protestants throughout the period of Reformation in the sixteenth century (and which continue on today). Here, Nevin throws in his lot decidedly with the Reformed churches in rejecting that unbelievers receive the reality signified in the Sacrament. While Christ is objectively present through the power of the Holy Spirit, without faith all that is received is the sacramental signs. So Calvin, *Institutes*, 4.17.33: "[T]his is the wholeness of the Sacrament, which the whole world cannot violate: that the flesh and blood of Christ are no less truly given to the unworthy than to God's elect believers. At the same time, it is true, however, that, just as rain falling upon a hard rock flows off because no entrance opens into the stone, the wicked by their hardness so repel God's grace that it does not reach them."

A *real* presence, in opposition to the notion that Christ's flesh and blood are not made present to the communicant in *any* way. A *spiritual* real presence, in opposition to the idea that Christ's body is in the elements in a local or corporal manner. Not real simply, and not spiritual simply; but real, and yet spiritual at the same time. The body of Christ is in heaven, the believer on earth; but by the power of the Holy Ghost, nevertheless, the obstacle of such vast local distance is fully overcome, so that in the sacramental act, while the outward symbols are received in an outward way, the very body and blood of Christ are at the same time inwardly and supernaturally communicated to the worthy receiver, for the real nourishment of his new life.[9]

---

9. Nevin, *Mystical Presence*, 56. It is vitally important to note here that when Nevin speaks of a "spiritual" presence of Christ in the Supper, he is not referring to a sort of disembodied presence of the Spirit of Christ, but rather to a real, substantial presence of the entire person Christ in both his divine and human natures brought about *by the operation of the Holy Spirit*, to be received by faith. This will be a key point at issue between Nevin and Hodge. To guard against misunderstanding, then, when one reads the term "spiritual" in Nevin (and no less in Calvin) with reference to the Eucharistic presence of Christ, one should read, *"by the operation of the Holy Spirit."* On this point, Nevin is a faithful expositor of Calvin's sacramental theology. In *Institutes* 4.17.33, for instance, Calvin writes, "For us the manner is spiritual because the secret power of the Spirit is the bond of our union with Christ" (1405). And in his *Clear Explanation* against Heshusius, Calvin writes that, "Although Christ is distant in respect of place, he is yet present by the boundless energy of his Spirit, so that his flesh can give us life" (*Theological Treatises*, 289). David Willis has thus aptly put it that, "For Calvin, to say that Christ is really present and that he is spiritually present are synonymous, since 'spiritually' refers to the action of the Holy Spirit who joins sign to reality and

Though Christ is in heaven and the assembly of believers on earth, the person of Christ himself, in both his divine and human natures, is substantially brought into the presence of the congregation by the power of the Holy Spirit. And although believers alone actually partake of the reality presented to them in the Sacrament, Christ is nevertheless offered to all to be received by faith. According to Nevin, due to the sacramental union between sign and reality, the grace offered in the rite is objective.[10]

From his statement of the doctrine, Nevin moves on to a historical treatment in order to prove that what he has set forth up to this point is indeed the Eucharistic doctrine that was held by the vast majority of Reformed churches in the sixteenth century. Here Nevin charts out his interpretation of the development of Reformed Eucharistic theology from the primitive years of the tradition toward its apex in the mind and writings of Calvin, concluding with the endorsement and ratification of Calvin's doctrine in the Reformed Confessions.

He begins his historical survey with some early confessional documents (such as the First Basel and First Helvetic confessions) and then moves from there into a demonstration of the doctrine of Calvin. Thereafter Nevin displays the widespread acceptance of Calvin's view of the Eucharist by the Reformed churches in the majority of Reformed Confessions that were penned during Calvin's day, also

---

community to Christ" (Willis, "A Reformed Doctrine of the Eucharist and Ministry," 295).

10. Nevin, *Mystical Presence*. 57.

adding into the mix some other individual early Reformed authorities for good measure.[11]

John Calvin appears as Nevin's highest ecclesiastical authority in the historical section, and this is by design, for he sees Calvin as the "great interpreter" and expounder of the faith of the Reformed churches: "No authority in the case can be entitled to greater respect. He was emphatically the great theologian of his age. On this point, moreover, he is clearly the organ and interpreter of the mind of the church, in whose bosom he stood."[12] The most prominent sources in Nevin's exposition of Calvin's Eucharistic theology come from book 4 of the *Institutes*, the Geneva Catechism, and Calvin's reply to the Lutheran Tileman Hesshusius.

But this Calvinistic doctrine of the holy Eucharist had all but vanished in the faith and life of the Reformed churches by the middle of the nineteenth century, and Nevin proceeds to exhibit and lament this abandonment. According to him, the difference between the doctrine of the sixteenth century Reformed churches on the Eucharist and the churches of the nineteenth century was "real and serious."[13] He locates the cause of this apostasy in the

11. Ibid., 59–98. Nevin finds confessional support in the Confession of Basel, art. 6; First Helvetic Confession, art. 20 and 23; Gallican Confession, art. 36–37; Old Scots Confession, art. 21; Belgic Confession, art. 33 and 35; Second Helvetic Confession, art. 21; Heidleberg Heidelberg Catechism, Q. 75, 76, and 79; Westminster Confession, 29. 7; Westminster Larger Catechism, Q. 168 and 170. Also playing a part in Nevin's historical treatment are Guilliame Farel, Theodore Beza, Peter Martyr Vermigli, Zacharias Ursinus, Rudolph Hospinian, Thomas Hooker, and John Owen.

12. Nevin, *Mystical Presence*, 63.

13. Ibid., 111.

widespread acceptance of what he labels "Puritanism"[14] and "Sectarianism." Both of these systems, according to Nevin, deny any unique grace to the Christian Sacraments, but rather view them as mere outward ordinances or devotional aids, and therefore are completely at odds with the profound, real, mystical conception of the original Reformed churches, which saw Eucharistic grace as unique. There is consequently a great conflict here between two different doctrines of the Eucharist and, in effect, two entirely different theological systems: "The two theories, it is clear, are different throughout. Nor is the difference such as may be considered of small account. It is not simply formal or accidental. The modern Puritan view evidently involves a material falling away, not merely from the old Calvinistic doctrine, but from its inward life and force."[15]

14. Nevin's use of the term "Puritan" is somewhat problematic historically. He did not have in mind in his use of this label a group of 17th century English non-conformist theologians. In fact, his use of certain "Puritan" theologians, such as John Owen, for historical support of his sacramental theology would seem to imply otherwise. And Nevin frequently uses the phrase "modern Puritan view," which would apply to theologians of his own day but not to 17th century English divines. What he does mean, rather, is an overall unchurchly and anti-sacramental way of viewing the Christian faith, which he considered to have pervaded the nineteenth century Reformed churches. In this regard, he probably has in mind in his use of the term "Puritan" something along the lines of what has come to be known as American Revivalism, not necessarily those writers who are widely referred to as "Puritans" today. Although in Nevin's assessment certain writers who might fall within the latter category probably would fit the bill of his pejorative label "Puritan," this is not the case across the board.

15. Nevin, *Mystical Presence*, 119.

After the historical groundwork has been laid, Nevin provides his own attempt at a "scientific statement" of the doctrine. Here he contends that Calvin's original exposition of the Lord's Supper, though essentially correct, is "embarrassed with some difficulties," and he accordingly sets out to correct these.[16] Nevin sees Calvin's doctrine as suffering from a "false psychology" which equates the human body with material volume. He offers as a corrective to this the idea of the body as a "system of life," which does not necessitate a materialistic conception of the human body. Thus, Nevin asserts, we are not bound when speaking of Christ's body to conceive of it simply in terms of material volume, but as the "organic law of Christ's human life."[17]

A second point at which Nevin seeks to reformulate Calvin's doctrine has to do with the Genevan Reformer's failure "to insist, with proper freedom and emphasis, on the absolute *unity* of what we denominate *person*"[18] Thus, according to Nevin, Calvin "dwells too much on the life-giving virtue of Christ's *flesh* simply." Nevin asserts that, rather than speaking primarily of the reception of Christ's *flesh* in the Eucharist, it is better to view the transaction as a communication of Christ's divine-human *life* flowing from his entire person to the entire persons of believers by the power of the Holy Ghost, who is one with Christ and brings the faithful into union with him.[19]

16. Ibid., 147.

17. Ibid., 148–49.

18. Ibid., 149.

19. Ibid., 149–50. Although Nevin seems to interpret him otherwise, Calvin likely has in view something close to this when he makes statements such as, "the flesh of Christ becomes vivifying to us, inas-

Third, Nevin contends that Calvin does not sufficiently distinguish between Christ's individual life and his generic life. Here he offers various analogies to explain what he means by "generic life," such as the union between an acorn and a tree. The acorn develops naturally into a tree, which tree then drops more acorns and eventually develops into a forest. Thus, acorn, tree, and forest are all invigorated and organically united by one and the same life shared by all the various manifestations of that life. Similarly, the divine-human life of Christ flows out from him (the vine) into his people (the branches).[20]

After providing the proper modifications to Calvin's Eucharistic theory, Nevin offers a systematic theological and biblical defense of the central doctrine of his system of thought—the mystical union between Christ and the

much as Christ, by the incomprehensible virtue of his Spirit, trans-fuses his own proper life into us from the substance of his flesh, so that he himself lives in us, and his life is common to us" (*Theological Treatises*, 267).

20. Nevin, *Mystical Presence*, 152. While Nevin (due to the influence of the German mediating theology on his thinking) utilizes this organic imagery to a much greater extent than can be found in any of the sixteenth century Reformers, it should be noted that such expressions are not entirely absent in Calvin. So, for instance, in the *Best Method of Obtaining Concord*: "Christ, by the incomprehensible virtue of his Spirit, infuses his life into us and makes it common to us, just as in a tree the vital sap diffuses itself from the root among the branches, or as vigour from the head spreads to the limbs" (*Theological Treatises*, 326).

An important thing to take note of in all three of Nevin's attempts to modify Calvin's doctrine is his indebtedness to nineteenth century German idealist modes of thought. This betrays Nevin's fundamentally mediating frame of mind: he is attempting to synthesize what he sees as the substance of historic Reformed doctrine with the best insights he could gather from nineteenth century German metaphysics.

Church. We will enter into a more thorough discussion of this section of the work in the next chapter. For our purposes here it is necessary to simply say a brief word about the place Scripture held in the formulation of Nevin's doctrine of the Eucharist, and also how Nevin's conception of the believer's union with Christ shaped his understanding of what takes place in the Sacrament.

Nevin had a comprehensive (one might say an "organic," to use his own preferred terminology) approach to biblical exegesis. He did not think that the validity of one's theological perspective stands or falls with an examination of isolated proof-texts. Accordingly, neither did he believe that debates over different theories of the Lord's Supper could be settled by simply marshalling forth interpretations of relevant passages such as the institution narratives. He therefore does not seek to offer any detailed exegetical analysis of these passages, as we might expect a Protestant theologian to do in a work attempting to prove a particular theory of the Eucharist. To be sure, he did have his interpretations of these passages, but he was quite clear about the fact that he was not concerned with proving his point by way of appeals to "clear Scripture." [21] Thus, rather than rooting his doctrine in a certain exegesis of specific passages, Nevin held that the overall biblical presentation of the mystical union between Christ and the Church forms the theological foundation for a proper understanding of what takes place in the Eucharist.

---

21. For an excellent and thorough treatment of Nevin's hermeneutic, see DiPuccio, *The Interior Sense of Scripture*. DiPuccio rightly describes Nevin's hermeneutic as "transcendental" and "mystical" (3).

According to Nevin, the union between believers and Christ is real and substantial—they share *one life*: "Christ communicates his own life substantially to the soul on which he acts, causing it to grow into his very nature. This is the *mystical union*; the basis of our whole salvation; the only medium by which it is possible for us to have an interest in the grace of Christ under any other view."[22] This union is wrought entirely by the Holy Ghost, and the new life in Christ is communicated to the soul through faith, ultimately culminating in the eschatological resurrection: "The old body becomes itself, in a mysterious way, the womb of a higher corporeity, the life-law of Christ's own glorious body; which is at last, through the process of death and the resurrection, set free from the first form of existence entirely, and made to supersede it for ever in the immortality of heaven."[23]

As is the case with the believer's reception of the life of Christ in the mystical union, the efficacy of the Sacrament is contingent upon the faith of the recipient, since faith is the instrument by which one receives Christ. However, grace is nonetheless objectively present, as sign and reality are mysteriously bound together by Christ's words of institution and the power of the Holy Ghost.[24] For a sacrament to truly be a sacrament there must be present both sign and reality existing in a real union. And due to this union, Christ is truly and objectively offered to all, to be received by faith.[25]

22. Nevin, *Mystical Presence*, 159.

23. Ibid., 167.

24. Ibid., 168.

25. So Calvin, in reply to Heshusius' assertion that his doctrine of the Eucharist did away with any objective presence of Christ: "[W]e

What is conveyed in the Eucharist is the peculiar benefit of Christ's once for all sacrifice, and the imputation of Christ's righteousness received by faith alone is the foundation for the communication of Christ's life to the believer. But, as has been previously stated, this imputation must be accompanied by a true communication of life if it is to have any real effect. And this is a blessing brought about uniquely in the Christian Eucharist.[26]

HODGE'S CRITIQUE

It took Charles Hodge two years to work up the motivation to plod through Nevin's argument in *The Mystical Presence*. His words explaining this fact at the beginning of his article in the *Princeton Review*, titled "The Doctrine of the Reformed Church on the Lord's Supper,"[27] betray a sense of fear for what he suspected he might find in the work penned by one of his most prized former students: "We have had Dr. Nevin's work on the 'Mystical Presence' on our table since its publication, some two years ago, but have never really read it, until within a fortnight. We do not suppose other people are quite as bad, in this respect, as ourselves. Our

maintain that in the Supper Christ holds forth his body to reprobates as well as to believers, but in such a manner that those who profane the Sacrament by unworthy receiving make no change in its nature, nor in any respect impair the effect of the promise. But although Christ remains like to himself and true to his promises, it does not follow that what is given is received by all indiscriminately" (In *Theological Treatises*, 283).

26. *Mystical Presence*, 169–74.

27. Originally printed in *The Biblical Repository and Princeton Review*, vol. XX, 1848, 227–78. Citations here, however, will follow the reprinted article in Hodge, *Essays and Reviews*, 341–92.

experience, however, has been that it requires the stimulus of a special necessity to carry us through such a book."[28]

Bard Thompson has suggested that these words imply that Hodge was "indisposed to the Eucharist."[29] This, however, is most likely not entirely accurate. There were very few topics that Charles Hodge did not take an interest in, and there is no indication in his other writings on the subject that he was disinclined to the Eucharist. The more plausible explanation is Hodge's continually expressed loathing of theological works from the perspective of what he called the "mystical school," especially the nineteenth century German mediating theologians. In this regard, noticing an essay placed at the beginning of Nevin's work by Dr. Ullmann from Heidelberg must not have produced in Hodge much desire to look into the book. And its very title no doubt sent off an alarm in his mind indicating that he would not be pleased with what he was going to find within it.

His reluctance aside, Hodge did nevertheless take it upon himself in 1848 to address the important issues raised by the theologian from Mercersburg. His review of *The Mystical Presence* consists of two sections. First, he deals specifically with Nevin's presentation of the Reformed doctrine of the Eucharist and the consequent charge against the Reformed churches of the nineteenth century of apostasy from this view. Second, he seeks to address the foundational anthropological and Christological tenets of Nevin's system as a whole as found in *The Mystical Presence*. We will look

28. Hodge, *Essays and Reviews*, 341.

29. Preface to Nevin, *The Mystical Presence and Other Writings*, 12.

at the second section in the next chapter. It is our concern here to focus only on the first portion of Hodge's review.

After expressing his distaste for Nevin's charge of apostasy from the Reformed faith, Hodge states that his purpose is to demonstrate the true doctrine of the Reformed church on the matter, and thereby to "give our reasons for thinking that Dr. Nevin is tenfold further from the doctrines of our common fathers, than those whom he commiserates and condemns."[30] While admitting that, "it is confessedly a very difficult matter to obtain clear views of what was the real doctrine of the Reformed church on the Lord's Supper in the sixteenth century,"[31] Hodge nevertheless proceeds to offer an approximation of what that doctrine was. He begins by agreeing with Nevin that one's view of the sacrament will always be dependent upon one's conception of union with Christ. He agrees also that this union is indeed a great mystery, even going so far as to say that "we are partakers of [Christ's] life," and that it "is in virtue of his assumption of our nature that he stands to us in the intimate relation now spoken of."[32] More than this, Hodge even agrees that the relation between believers and Christ is according to body as well as soul, and states that "This union was always represented as a real union, not merely imaginary or simply moral, nor arising from the mere benefits which Christ has procured."[33]

Hodge then begins to articulate the points on which he disagrees with Nevin. He contends that the whole

30. Hodge, *Essays and Reviews*, 341–42.

31. Ibid., 342.

32. Ibid., 342.

33. Ibid., 343.

Reformed church of the sixteenth century denied the "actual reception and manducation of the real body of Christ." On the contrary, "all the Reformed answered" that the manner in which the reception of Christ in the Supper is to be understood is that believers receive the "virtue or efficacy" of Christ's once for all sacrifice upon the cross.[34] According to Hodge, though there were a variety of ways this truth was expressed by Reformed theologians in the sixteenth century, none of them in reality pressed beyond this fundamentally unphysical conception of the reception of Christ in the Sacrament.

Hodge does however admit that some of the expressions used by various theologians (such as Calvin) and the Reformed confessions can tend to be somewhat confusing. But he claims that this is understandable if we realize that the reason for such manners of expression was the desire of the Reformed churches to conciliate with the Lutherans. The Reformed, Hodge tells us, spoke in ways they normally would not have were it not for this ecumenical concern: "It is not wonderful, therefore, that their language should, at times, be hard to reconcile with what was in fact the real doctrine of the Reformed church . . . And we find, in fact, that as soon as this pressure from without was removed, all ambiguity as to the Reformed doctrine of the Lord's Supper ceased."[35]

Hodge's historical examination is shaped by the contention that there were three basic forms which the Reformed doctrine of the Eucharist took: 1. The memorialism of the early Helvetic churches led by Zwingli and Oecolampadius, 2. The spiritual, but real, reception of Christ spoken of by

34. Ibid.
35. Ibid., 344.

Calvin, and 3. A position that struck a *via media* between these two ends of the Reformed spectrum. Hodge categorizes each of the major Reformed Confessions according to these three different views.[36] In the first category he places the Zurich confessions, the Tetrapolitan Confession, the First Basel Confession, and the First Helvetic Confession. In the second category he places The Gallican Confession, the 39 Articles, the Old Scottish Confession, and the Belgic Confession. In the third category he places the *Consensus Tigurinus* (of which he provides a lengthier treatment than the others), the Heidleberg Catechism, and the Second Helvetic Confession.

It is the last of these three categories of confessions that Hodge argues to be the most authoritative, as they represent the solidification of the understanding of the Reformed churches on the issue and the final compromise between the groups that held to the other two views.[37] It should also be noted that, regarding Calvin's view, Hodge charges Nevin with misrepresentation of the facts, accusing him of offering only selective quotations. This is merely asserted, however. Hodge provides no passages from Calvin that would contradict Nevin's presentation.[38]

36. Ibid., 345–56. While siding with Nevin for the most part as to the historical points of this controversy, B. A. Gerrish is in agreement with Hodge's contention that there were three views held by the Reformed in the sixteenth century. He has helpfully labeled these three views "Symbolic Memorialism," "Symbolic Instrumentalism," and "Symbolic Parallelism," respectively. See his excellent treatment on *The Lord's Supper in the Reformed Confessions*, 239.

37. Hodge, *Essays and Reviews*, 355–56.

38. Ibid., 348.

After laying down his primary historical points, Hodge goes on to address the specific features of the doctrine of the Reformed churches on the Lord's Supper. According to Hodge, Christ is present in the Sacrament only by way of virtue and efficacy, but not substantially in both his divinity *and* humanity. Under this conception, Christ is spiritually present to the mind of the believer: "There is, therefore, a presence of Christ's body in the Lord's Supper; not local, but spiritual; not for the senses but for the mind and to faith; not of nearness but of efficacy."[39]

According to Hodge, when the Reformed speak of "eating" and "drinking," they mean these terms to be understood as synonymous with faith itself. He admits that Calvin distinguished between eating and believing, but seems to think his view was only a private opinion and declares that

39. Ibid., 360. Hodge states also in volume 3 of his *Systematic Theology*: "The body and blood are near us when they fill our thoughts, are apprehended by faith as broken and shed for our salvation, and exert upon us their proper effect" (642). Here we may note again the difference between Nevin and Hodge with regard to what they mean by the phrase "spiritual presence." Much to the contrary of Nevin's understanding of the term "spiritual" with reference to Christ's presence in the Eucharist, when Hodge speaks of a "spiritual presence," he does in fact seem to mean something like "non-substantial" or, perhaps better, "according to the divine nature only." Evans has noted the influence of Hodge's Common Sense metaphysic on this point: "The denial of a 'local presence' is indeed a distinctive of Reformed theology, but while Calvin and Nevin sought to understand how Christ's humanity might be present in a non-local and spiritual mode, Hodge concluded that no realistic presence existed, only a presence of 'efficacy and virtue. ' This was a point where his Scottish Common Sense metaphysic largely determined his conclusion. For Hodge, body and blood are material substances, and to speak of body and blood as actually present in a non-material and non-local mode is sheer nonsense" (*Imputation and Impartation*, 350).

there is no "force" behind the distinction.[40] There is in reality no difference at all between "eating" the body of Christ in the Supper and the ordinary act of believing. Thus, there is nothing *unique* in the Eucharist which cannot be received by the believer elsewhere: "The question, whether . . . there is any special benefit or communion with Christ to be had there, and which cannot elsewhere be obtained . . . the Reformed unanimously [answer] in the negative."[41]

By the use of the terms "body" and "blood" in speaking of the sacrament, the Reformed mean, Hodge tells us:

> the virtue, efficacy, or life-giving power of his body. But there are two ways in which this was understood. Some intended by it, not the virtue of Christ's body and blood as flesh and blood, but . . . their sacrificial, atoning efficacy. Others insisted that besides this there was a vivifying efficacy imparted to the body of Christ by its union with the divine nature, and that by the power of the Holy Ghost, the believer in the Lord's Supper

40. Hodge, *Essays and Reviews*, 361.

41. Ibid., 361–62. While this is somewhat overstated (in that the "elsewhere" tended to be confined by the sixteenth century Reformed specifically to the preaching of the gospel), Hodge is essentially correct on this last point. For Calvin, Christ is made present and offered in the preaching of the gospel as well as in the administration of the sacraments. The sacraments hold out the same promise as is offered in the word preached—Christ with all his benefits—although they do this in a more profound way: "God gives no more by visible signs than by his Word, but gives it in a different manner, because our weakness stands in need of a variety of helps" (Calvin, *Theological Treatises*, 281). However, this is the case because, for Calvin, the preaching of the gospel is itself sacramental in nature. For an excellent modern Reformed exposition of the sacramental nature of the preaching of the gospel, see Horton, *People and Place*, 37–51.

and elsewhere, received into his soul by faith this
mysterious and supernatural influence.[42]

He claims that both of these views are acceptable in
the Reformed tradition, as those holding to either understanding never broke fellowship with those holding the
other view. "But," Hodge continues, "if a decision must be
made between them, the higher authority is certainly due to
the doctrine of sacrificial efficacy first mentioned."[43]

He reaches this conclusion because first, according to
him, the authority of the *Consensus Tigurinus*, the Second
Helvetic Confession, and the Heidleberg Catechism "out-
weigh the private authority of Calvin or the dubious expressions of the Gallican, Belgic, and some minor Confessions."[44]
And second, the latter view is considered by him to be more
consistent with the Reformed system of doctrine as a whole,
primarily with regard to the fact that it had always been the
consensus opinion of the Reformed that there is no benefit
that believers enjoy after the incarnation which they did not
receive before it.[45]

The effect of receiving the sacrament by faith is "union
with Christ, and the consequent reception of his benefits,"
but the sacraments convey nothing unique which may not
be had without them.[46] Hodge sums up his understanding of the doctrine of the Reformed church on the Lord's
Supper in this manner:

42. Hodge, *Essays and Reviews*, 363.
43. Ibid., 365.
44. Ibid.
45. Ibid., 365–66.
46. Ibid., 368–72.

> Christ is really present to his people, in this or-
> dinance, not bodily, but by his Spirit; not in the
> sense of local nearness, but of efficacious op-
> eration. They receive him, not with the mouth,
> but by faith; they receive his flesh, not as flesh,
> not as material particles, nor its human life, but
> his body as broken and his blood as shed. The
> union thus signified and effected, between him
> and them is not a corporeal union, nor a mixture
> of substances, but spiritual and mystical, arising
> from the indwelling of the Spirit. The efficacy of
> this sacrament is . . . solely in the attending influ-
> ence of the Holy Ghost.[47]

Consequently, Hodge thrusts back at Nevin the very same charge which Nevin in *The Mystical Presence* had leveled against the majority of the Reformed churches of nineteenth century America—apostasy from the doctrine of the Reformed Confessions on the Lord's Supper. In this regard, Hodge accused Nevin of choosing his historical authorities selectively and with citing them incompletely. He also believed that Nevin had simply glossed over the variation of opinion on Christ's presence in the Eucharist that existed between the original Reformed theologians and Confessions themselves. As for the substantial points, Hodge considered it to be Nevin who was deviating from the original Reformed doctrine of the Lord's Supper in his con-tention that Christ is substantially present in the Eucharist in *both* his divine *and* human natures, and in his insistence on the communication of the entire Christ, in both his di-vine and human natures, to the believer. To Charles Hodge

47. Ibid., 372–73. Notice especially the statement, "*not bodily, but by his Spirit.*"

and many other nineteenth century Presbyterians like him, the views of theologians such as John Williamson Nevin represented "a radical rejection" of the Eucharistic doctrine of the original Reformed churches.[48]

NEVIN'S HISTORICAL DEFENSE

James Turner has said that "Hodge could speak with greater authority than most of his interlocutors for the very good reason that he *knew* more than they did."[49] This was no doubt true in most situations, but in the case of John Williamson Nevin, he had chosen to engage one man whom he simply did not *know* more than, at least with regard to a discussion centered on the interpretation of historical documents.

After noticing Hodge's scathing review, Nevin had little choice but to defend himself, for, as James Hasting Nichols notes, he "recognized in his former teacher his most formidable theological opponent."[50] And so Nevin went on what may justly be called a war path, tracking down every single nuance of Hodge's historical presentation and seeking to utterly demolish it. The end result was a compilation of historical arguments and citations that developed into an article of no less than one hundred twenty six pages in length, which appeared in the 1850 volume of the *Mercersburg Review*. The title that Nevin chose for the article is the same title

---

48. Ibid., 373.

49. Turner, "Charles Hodge in the Intellectual Weather of the Nineteenth Century" (in *Charles Hodge Revisited*, edited by Stewart and Morehead, 41–61), 43.

50. Nichols, *Romanticism in American Theology*, 141.

Hodge gave to his critique: "The Doctrine of the Reformed Church on the Lord's Supper."[51]

Nevin states that his purpose in this article is "primarily altogether historical," and tells us that he is seeking only to defend his contention concerning what the true doctrine of the Reformed church originally was. According to him, Hodge's review was "the only respectable or tolerable attempt yet made to set aside the historical representation contained in the *The Mystical Presence*."[52] "Tolerable" was probably as charitable a word as Nevin could muster up, for he was no doubt appalled by the dismissive manner in which his thoroughly researched and carefully set forth historical presentation of the topic was treated by his former professor. The article is composed of three sections: 1. a restatement of Nevin's Eucharistic doctrine as it originally appeared in the early pages of *The Mystical Presence*,[53] 2. a counterstatement to Hodge's counterstatement, and 3. a historical trial and analysis of the various source materials relevant to the discussion.

After providing the restatement of his doctrine, Nevin begins his counterassault by going through and answering in order each of Hodge's points about the doctrine of the Reformed church on the Lord's Supper. At the outset of his counterstatement, Nevin charges that Hodge did not even

51. Citations here will follow the republication of the article in Nevin, *The Mystical Presence and other Writings on the Eucharist* (edited by Thompson and Bricker).

52. Nevin, *Writings on the Eucharist*, 267.

53. The reprinted portion of *The Mystical Presence* appears in the original article in the *Mercersburg Review*, but is not contained in the *Writings on the Eucharist* volume, as the same volume itself contains a reprinting of *The Mystical Presence*.

pretend "to enter into any extended or exact historical criticism in the case. He proposes simply to take up the whole subject in an ex cathedra general way, lumping the authorities to suit his own mind, and ruling their testimony thus to such results as the investigation in his judgment is felt to require."[54]

He then criticizes Hodge for making an issue of the disparity among the early Reformed and thereby claiming that we can come to no firm conclusion on what is the proper doctrine of the Reformed tradition. He charges Hodge with making this claim "for the very purpose of feeling himself more at liberty thus to construct from its chaotic material an answer to please his own taste."[55]

Thus, we have here a criticism of Hodge's basic historical method which demonstrates that Nevin, for his part, was quite aware of the foundational differences between himself and Hodge at the level of methodology. This is a criticism he would level against any use of sources, whether biblical or historical, that would presume to marshal forth bare citations as though the materials were simply a "storehouse of facts," or little other than a mass of proof-texts.[56] Few historical presentations could have been more averse to Nevin's refined Hegelianism, for when Nevin looked at historical data, he was not content to just take out of it what he saw as adequate to prove a point (though, of course, he certainly had his biases and points to prove). Rather, he

54. Nevin, *Writings on the Eucharist*, 271.

55. Ibid., 273.

56. Nichols has claimed that for Hodge, "the past was an armory of theological tenets, and a man had a right to pick and choose as he would" (*Romanticism in American Theology*, 90).

labored to see the genuine movement of history (and espe-cially the history of ideas) in an attempt to, in a sense, enter into its *life*. Peter Wallace is therefore correct in his assess-ment that, "At the root of their debate lies an irreconcilable difference over the nature of history."[57]

With his preliminary rebuttal of Hodge's historical method taken care of, Nevin proceeds to claim that many of Hodge's points in themselves do not touch on any sig-nificant difference between Hodge's understanding of Reformed Eucharistic theology and the doctrine presented in *The Mystical Presence*. In this regard, Nevin complains that Hodge has poisoned the well by presenting the case at every point as though Nevin disagrees with what are obvi-ous facts, "covertly implying at least that the positions it sets aside, in each case, belong fairly and truly to the opposite cause."[58] For instance, to the contention that the Reformed believed that Christ is present in virtue and efficacy, but not corporeally or locally, Nevin says that "there is not a word in *The Mystical Presence* . . . that can be said to affirm what is here denied, or to deny what is here affirmed." He grants also that the original Reformed doctrine was one of a spiri-tual, non-corporeal eating by faith whereby the believer re-ceives Christ's body and blood into the soul by the power of the Holy Spirit. Much less had Nevin ever contended that the "material particles of Christ's body" were thought by the Reformed to be received in the Eucharist.[59] However, he

---

57. Wallace, "History and Sacrament," 177.

58. Nevin, *Writings on the Eucharist*, 273–76.

59. In *The Mystical Presence*, Nevin had clearly stated that, by the "real communication of Christ's life to the believer," he *did not* mean "that the material particles of Christ's life are supposed to be carried

does object to the idea, to which Hodge seems bound, that there can only be two senses of "presence": one material to the senses, the other spiritual and immaterial to the mind only. "But," says Nevin, "The Calvinistic doctrine . . . never opposes a simply intellectual presence to a gross sensible presence, but holds either of these . . . to be a presence in the sphere of mere nature and flesh." Also, Nevin does admit the truth of Hodge's point that there was a difference of opinion in the earliest days of the Reformed churches, but he objects to siding with one over the other.[60]

Although the two men are agreed that union with Christ is a blessing brought about in the Lord's Supper, Nevin objects to Hodge's unwillingness to interpret this union in what he sees as its most natural meaning—that believers are really and truly united with the divine-human life of Christ and partake of that life by the power of the Holy Spirit.[61] Similarly, while agreeing with Hodge that the Sacraments are efficacious means of grace which have their efficacy not in themselves, nor in the one administering them, but rather in the operation of the Holy Spirit, Nevin takes issue with the Princeton theologian's tendency to equate the Sacrament with the elements. In the historic Reformed understanding, a Sacrament includes both sign *and* reality, which cannot be separated from each other. Therefore, to speak of the Sacrament as something wholly earthly, devoid of the presence of Christ, is to offer an en-

---

over, by this supernatural process, into the believer's person" (56).

60. Nevin, *Writings on the Eucharist*, 282.

61. Ibid., 284.

tirely different conception of a Sacrament than what the Reformed confessions set down.[62]

To Hodge's claim that the view of Calvin concerning the vivifying power of Christ's flesh was a foreign element introduced into the Reformed doctrine, Nevin holds firm in his contention that the opposite is in fact the case, and that the "Puritan" view is the foreign element which crept in unawares: "That a change has taken place in later times we do not deny. But this, we contend, has been for the worse and not for the better." Nevin denies too the claim that the Reformed churches merely asserted a general presence of Christ's divine nature, thereby "resolving it altogether into a simply mental presence." Thus, Nevin rejects Hodge's assertion that the Reformed view excluded any participation in the human side of Christ's life: "the doctrine in question never set aside the true meaning of the incarnation in any such Gnostic style."[63] The agency of the Holy Spirit in the sacramental transaction does not necessarily exclude "Christ's proper presence," as Hodge seems to claim, for, as Nevin tells us, "this whole construction . . . is false and wrong. The intervention of the Spirit . . . stands opposed only to the idea of all action that falls within the sphere of mere nature, and was never designed to be set in this way over against the reality of Christ's presence." Finally, the idea that the Reformed view holds to no special grace in the sacraments themselves is also contested by Nevin: "We affirm on the contrary that the Reformers—with the whole ancient church—acknowledge a real conjunction between the outward form of the sacraments and their inward grace.

62. Ibid., 285–86.
63. Ibid., 291–92.

The latter was taken to belong to their very constitution as truly as the first . . . not, of course, in the outward elements or signs in themselves considered, but in the transaction taken as a whole."[64]

Next on Nevin's agenda is an exhaustive historical defense of his counterpoints. At nearly one hundred pages in length, however, a full treatment of his use and interpretation of sources is not within the scope of this chapter. It will suffice to note some of his most foundational arguments.

While conceding to Hodge that there were two views of the Eucharist held in the sixteenth century, Nevin argues that Calvin's doctrine is the mature completion of the primitive view held by Zwingli: "The Reformed doctrine starts in Switzerland under the first aspect, but completes itself finally through Calvin, under the second; not in such a way as to drop the old view, but so as to bring it to its full significance, by joining it to its proper basis in the other. *This union of the two views forms the true sacramental creed of the Reformed Church, as it appears in all the later confessions.*"[65] Here we may notice the Hegelian tendency of Nevin's historiography. He interprets the history of early Reformed Eucharistic theology as a development and synthesis of two different theories into one in the later confessions. It is also important to recognize, however, that the two conceptions of the Eucharist which are said to be joined together in the later confessions are not seen by Nevin as antithetical to each other, but rather as complimentary.

Thus, Nevin's historiography of the Reformation sources is an endeavor to understand the movement of

64. Ibid., 293–94.
65. Ibid., 295.

ideas toward a completed synthesis. He finds this synthesis in the Eucharistic thought of John Calvin, which is ratified in the later sixteenth century Reformed Confessions. As Nevin sees it, Hodge's method is quite contrary to this: "The Princeton view, as we have seen, bases [its] representation not so much on history but on its own sense of theological propriety."[66] Hodge's "sense of theological propriety" that Nevin has in mind here is his assumption of the supposed superiority of the "sacrificial view" of the Eucharist and the idea that anything speaking of a communication of Christ's divine-human *life* is nonsense, along with the consequent assumption that the former theory must cancel out the latter, as the two are contradictory, not complementary. In opposition to this Princeton construction, Nevin argues that the two views are in fact complementary rather than contradictory, and that the former finds its completion in the latter.

Nevin further objects to Hodge's handling of the Reformed Confessions, considering his treatment to be arbitrary at best. It is not that Hodge was trying to willingly deceive his readers; he just did not consider the possibility that he may have been mistaken. He therefore read his own understanding of what must have been the case into the historical record. Nevin regards it as arbitrary in the extreme for Hodge to make the primitive form of Reformed doctrine take precedent over the more highly developed view seen in Calvin:

> The only proper classification of the confessions
> is into those before Calvin and those that fol-

66. Ibid., 296.

> low, and the only proper relation between the
> two classes is that which subordinates the first
> entirely to the second, as the acknowledged
> consummation at last of the whole confessional
> process. The earlier symbols lost their authority,
> in fact, with the appearance of the later Gallican,
> Scottish, Belgic, and Second Helvetic confes-
> sions, and the Heidelberg Catechism.[67]

This is really the fundamental issue between Nevin
and Hodge with regard to their interpretation of the historical data. Nevin's philosophy of history demanded unity,
development, and growth, while Hodge showed a tendency
to interpret the historical documents in isolation from each
other.

Whereas Hodge had interpreted Calvin through
the statements of the *Consensus Tigurinus*, Nevin considers it to be a more sound method to rely on the doctrine
found in Calvin's fuller and more systematic treatments of
his Eucharistic theology for a proper interpretation of the
Consensus. Concerning the interpretation of this document, Nevin states:

> These articles go as far as the case could possibly
> allow toward the Helvetic side . . . But it is not
> true that they involve . . . an abandonment of the
> ground previously held by Calvin in Strasbourg
> and Geneva. On the contrary, they show the
> triumph of Calvinism over what was still defec-
> tive in the old Swiss view . . . It is Bullinger who
> rises above his old position . . . in free obedience
> to the superior mind of Calvin, not Calvin that

67. Ibid., 300.

descends—as the *Princeton Review* would seem
to imagine.[68]

Thus, Nevin argues that according to the terminology
of the times, the *Consensus* was by no means articulating
the same doctrine as Hodge advocates: "All that the case
requires is that the document should be interpreted according to the *usus loquendi* of the sixteenth century, and not
after the sound it carries to merely modern ears."[69] Terms
such as "sign" and "signify," for instance, always included
the conviction in Calvin's mind (and among the sixteenth
century Reformed generally) in the actual presence of the
reality signified. And this also conditions the description of
the sacraments as "seals," concerning which Nevin states:

68. Ibid., 324. Nevin probably overstated his case on this point.
Paul Rorem, in his helpful essay, *The Consensus Tigurinus: Did
Calvin Compromise?*, rightly points out that while Calvin did later—
in his controversies with the Lutheran theologians Westphal and
Heshussius—provide an interpretation of the *Consensus* that was
entirely in line with his own doctrine, the correspondence between
Calvin and Bullinger indicates that both men compromised somewhat
in the terminology used in the document. Rorem seems correct in his
contention concerning the *Consensus* that "the absence of terminology
of 'instrument,' of 'through the sacrament,' and of 'presenting/offering'
(*exhibeo*) indicates Calvin's concession by omission." Rorem also notes
that in correspondence with Bucer, Calvin laments this omission.
(Rorem, "The Consensus Tigurinus," 89.)

69. Nevin, *Writings on the Eucharist*, 325. Concerning the use of
terms: although Hodge never formally responded to Nevin's article,
this particular insight does seem to be at least somewhat heeded by
him in volume 3 of his *Systematic Theology*, where he states: "It is
a very difficult matter to give an account of the Reformed doctrine
of the Lord's Supper satisfactory to all parties. This difficulty arises
partly from the fact that words have changed their meaning since the
days of the Reformation" (626).

"Dr. Hodge refers the idea of *sealing*, no doubt, to the general grace of God as proclaimed in the gospel. But it lies in the whole doctrine of Calvin . . . and also in the phraseology of the age, that it should be taken in the sense of an authentication of what is at hand mystically in the sacramental transaction itself."[70]

Nevin then goes on to provide a lengthy and detailed historical narrative of the relations between the early Reformed with the early Lutheran party. He views Zwingli as a sort of antithesis to Luther, and takes issue with Hodge's contention that the Reformed in these days showed any tendency to speak out of character from a desire to conciliate with the great Reformer of Wittenberg. Martin Bucer, it is true, made many attempts to convince the Swiss to accept his ambiguous terms as their own, but they were far from accepting this proposal: "Honest Helvetians! How little

---

70. Nevin, *Writings on the Eucharist*, 326. Calvin himself had argued in his *Short Treatise on the Lord's Supper* that "the sacraments of the Lord ought not and cannot at all be separated from their substance. To distinguish them so that they be not confused is not only good and reasonable but wholly necessary. But to divide them so as to set them up the one without the other is absurd" (147–48). On this point, B. A. Gerrish has contended that "Zwingli and Calvin held two totally different views of religious symbolism. Because the nature of the symbolical is not simply a fourth ingredient, but the total context of sacramental theology, it follows that even the verbal agreements of Zwingli and Calvin are totally qualified, and may conceal actual disagreement. Hence, though both can detect the same 'analogies' in Baptism and the Lord's Supper, the disagreement between the two men is more fundamental than their agreements, and puts Calvin in Luther's side of the line, not Zwingli's. For in Calvin's view it is the nature of the sacraments to cause and communicate (*apporter et communiquer*) what they signify" ("The Lord's Supper in the Reformed Confessions," 230).

evidence we see in all these transactions of a disposition to 'conciliate Luther,' at the cost of truth and sincerity . . . according to the general charge preferred by Dr. Hodge, against the whole Reformed Church in this period."[71] After these attempts were made by Bucer, the Swiss clarified their position, which clarification was strangely accepted by Luther. Nevin then argues that it is the period of calm that came after this conciliation during which the true meaning of the Reformed view was parsed out by Calvin and Melanchthon. In the minds of these two great theologians, we see a synthesis of what was essential to both Luther and Zwingli: "Megandrian Zwinglianism and Flacian Lutheranism are the opposite sides of the old antithesis, refusing to follow now the stream of history toward a true union of these divided interests in a higher view. That higher view, as it comes out at last in its full proportions, may be denominated Melanchthonian Calvinism."[72]

Nevin provides also a rather detailed historical treatment of Calvin's theory, which is similar in all essential points to what he had already offered in *The Mystical Presence*, only now bolstered by a much wider variety of citations and proofs. Especially pertinent here is the detailed presentation Nevin offers of Calvin's interaction with the Lutheran Joachim Westphal, a debate which was carried on by the two men between 1553 and 1557, and in which the *Consensus Tigurinus* occupies a place of central importance, as it was upon reading this document that Westphal took it upon himself to level his assault against Calvin's doctrine. Thus, as Nevin sees it, we have in this interaction

71. Nevin, *Writings on the Eucharist*, 309.
72. Ibid., 315.

between Calvin and Westphal an excellent body of material for a proper interpretation of Calvin's meaning in the *Consensus*.

Nevin charges Hodge with treating Calvin the same way Westphal and other extreme Lutherans did by charging him with inconsistencies and equivocations: "In both directions, it has been insisted that [Calvin] played an adroit game, stretched his own convictions to please the Lutherans, paltered in double senses and ambiguous terms, involved himself in contradictions, and took refuge in unintelligible distinctions. Westphal calls him an 'eel,' which no one could hold by the tail. Dr. Hodge is more respectful, but it comes to much the same thing at last."[73] He then asserts that, "One of the very best replies to Princeton, so far as Calvin is concerned, would be simply a full republication, in clear intelligible English, of his memorable Second Defense *Adversus Joachimi Westphali Calumnias*."[74] After this, he goes on to chastise Hodge and others for claiming that Calvin's theory is confused and hard to understand: "It is fashionable in certain quarters, we know, to speak of it as strangely confused and hard to comprehend. But there is no room for any such charge in the Calvinistic theory itself. All we need is to lay aside our stubborn preconceptions, and converse with it under its own form and on its own ground. Then all will become clear enough. It is only the medium through which it is viewed, that serves so often to wrap it in haze and mist."[75]

73. Ibid., 333.

74. Ibid.

75. Ibid., 343–44.

Nevin then offers three important insights which serve to clarify Calvin's doctrine. First, he explains what Calvin means when he speaks of the "life-giving virtue" of Christ's body: "By the life-giving virtue or efficacy of Christ's body, Calvin means always the very substance of Christ's life itself under its divine *human* form."[76] Second, when Calvin speaks of the "ascent" of the believer toward heaven in the sacrament, he is not referring to a mental ascent brought about by pious thoughts. Rather, "this refers merely to the order of the mystery here brought to pass, as something that transcends wholly all natural experience. He could not mean by it a simple act of thought, mounting upward to Christ in heaven, for that would reduce all to gross subjectivity which he continually disclaims."[77] Third, Nevin points out that when Calvin uses the term "spiritual" with reference to the presence of Christ in the sacrament, he is referring "only" to "the mode of the mystery, not the fact of the mystery itself." That is, he is speaking of a presence of the whole Christ brought about by the operation of the Holy Spirit, not a sort of disembodied presence of Christ's Spirit. He then quotes the Genevan Reformer as saying: "the body of Christ is said to be given spiritually in the Supper because the *secret energy of the Holy Spirit* causes things that are separated by local distance to be, notwithstanding, joined together, so that life is made to reach into us from heaven out of the flesh of Christ."[78]

Based on his detailed exposition of Calvin's doctrine, Nevin proceeds to enter into an exposition of the sixteenth

76. Ibid., 350.
77. Ibid., 351.
78. Ibid., 352.

century Reformed Confessions which made their appear-
ance after Calvin's doctrine had become well known and
widely disseminated. According to Nevin, once we have a
proper understanding of Calvin's doctrine, his use of sacramental terminology, and his universal acceptance as the
main authority of the Reformed churches in the latter half of
the sixteenth century, the meaning of these documents can
be arrived at in no uncertain terms. Nevin claims that it is
here that "we may see how altogether unhistorical is the form
in which the *Princeton Review* has seen fit to bring forward
its authorities, for the settlement of the general question in
debate."[79] The later sixteenth century Reformed confessions
demonstrate the full completion of the Reformed doctrine:
"Dr. Hodge's *third* class, in which he pretends to find a sort of
outward compromise between Calvinism and Zwinglianism
(this last taken in *his* Megandrian sense) is very much the
creature of his own imagination. The Heidleberg Catechism
. . . is decidedly Calvinistic; the *Consensus Tigurinus* was
considered to be so by Calvin himself; the Second Helvetic
Confession must be interpreted in the same way."[80] Nevin
views the Gallican, Old Scottish, Belgic, Second Helvetic,
and the Heidelberg Catechism as the most authoritative
Reformed confessions, because they mark the "completed
stage" of Reformed confessional orthodoxy and thus over-
shadow all earlier confessional documents. He then provides
a detailed analysis of the relevant portions of these confessions, all of which appeared from 1559–63, at the very height
of Calvin's influence.[81]

79. Ibid., 359.
80. Ibid., 360.
81. The final edition of Calvin's *Institutes* was published in 1559.

The final verdict of Nevin's historical analysis is that all of the authoritative Reformed Confessions from the period of 1559–63 represent the final synthesis between the sacrificial, memorial emphasis of Zwingli with the more developed view of Calvin that called attention to the actual presence and communication of the life-giving flesh of Christ by the Spirit. Rather than being simply a compromise between the two positions and surrendering something from each, as Hodge had asserted, Nevin contends that these documents provide us with the fully developed Reformed doctrine which retains what was essential to both streams of Reformed Eucharistic thought.

Confident that his detailed historical presentation has conclusively demonstrated the truth of the matter, Nevin's article is concluded with a brief analysis of the words of some of his contemporaries on the Eucharist—particularly Moses Stuart and John Dick—which reveal the variance between them and the Eucharistic doctrine of the sixteenth century Reformed Confessions. In this way, Nevin leaves little doubt that he remains fully convinced of his original thesis in *The Mystical Presence* concerning the widespread apostasy of nineteenth century Reformed theologians from the sixteenth century Reformed doctrine of the Eucharist. The words quoted by Nevin from John Dick's *Lectures on Theology* are especially noteworthy in this regard: "Now, a sign is very far from implying that the thing signified is present. It is rather understood to represent an absent object. Instead of being a fair conclusion from the Words of Institution, that there is a peculiar, mysterious presence of our Savior . . . it might rather be inferred that he is not present at all, and that the design of the symbols is to call him to remembrance in his absence."[82] In light of Nevin's historical analysis, such a conception would seem to have been the exact opposite of what the later sixteenth century Reformed confessions originally meant when they spoke of sacramental signs. At the very least, it is a far cry from the understanding of sacramental symbols set forth by Calvin:

> For unless a man means to call God a deceiver, he would never dare assert that an empty symbol is set forth by him. Therefore, if the Lord truly represents the participation in his body through the breaking of bread, there ought not to be the least doubt that he truly presents and shows his body. And the godly ought by all means to keep this rule: whenever they see symbols appointed by the Lord, to think and be persuaded that the truth of the thing signified is surely present there.[83]

Hence, it may be concluded that Nevin was quite justified in his lamentation of an apostasy in the nineteenth century from this original Calvinistic doctrine of the Holy Eucharist. Even if he may have stressed the extent of this falling away to an unwarranted degree, it is nevertheless apparent that there was a wide difference between sixteenth century Reformed sacramental theology and the sacra-

82. Quoted in Nevin, *Mystical Presence*, 393. The original citation is in John Dick, *Lectures on Theology, vol. 2*, 414. Dick's *Lectures on Theology* was utilized widely in theology courses in American Seminaries during the mid-nineteenth century—even by John Nevin at Mercersburg. In his section on the Lord's Supper, Dick grounds the presence of Christ in the Eucharist in Christ's general promise of his presence in Matt. 18. 20, which "relates to all his ordinances together without any special respect to the supper" (414).

83. Calvin, *Institutes*, 4.17.10.

mentology that had come to dominate the thinking of the majority of nineteenth century Reformed churches.[84]

CONCLUDING REMARKS

John Williamson Nevin conceived of the Eucharist as central to the entire system of Christian doctrine. In it, Christ's divine-human life is truly communicated to the believing recipient through the powerful operation of the Holy Spirit, who makes Christ really and substantially present in the sacrament to be received by faith through the act of eating and drinking consecrated bread and wine. Nevin argued that this is nothing more than the original Reformed doctrine of the Lord's Supper as formulated by John Calvin and set down by the most authoritative Reformed confessions of the sixteenth century, and that the majority of the Reformed churches in the nineteenth century had undergone a widespread apostasy from this view.

Charles Hodge retorted that Nevin was mistaken in his understanding of the original Reformed doctrine and therefore was consequently also misguided in his charge of apostasy. According to Hodge, there were two basic views initially held by the original Reformed churches on the Eucharist: one centering on the efficacy of Christ's once for all sacrifice on the cross, the other adding to this

84. Certain high church Southern Presbyterians, such as James Henley Thornwell and John Adger, are notable exceptions in this regard. See particularly Adger's article, "Calvin Defended Against Drs. Cunningham and Hodge." E. Brooks Holifield draws interesting connections between the controversy between Nevin and Hodge and similar differences among nineteenth century Southern Presbyterian theologians in "Mercersburg, Princeton, and the South."

an actual participation in Christ's life. The latter of these is the view held by Calvin. Yet, even here, there was never considered to be any real presence Christ in his *humanity*, but simply of efficacy and virtue. Hodge then interpreted the later Reformed Confessions as a compromise between those holding to Calvin's view and those holding to the view of Zwingli. And Hodge views this doctrine, which he supposed to have done away with the objectionable points in Calvin's formulation, as the true Reformed understanding.

Nevin responded by pointing out that Hodge's use of the historical sources was misguided, inaccurate, and conditioned by a false view of history which tended to treat historical data as a mere collection of isolated facts. He demonstrated this by providing a detailed historical defense of the development of Reformed Eucharistic doctrine from its earliest days toward its climax in the mind of Calvin and the eventual dissemination and acceptance of this Calvinistic view as seen in the authoritative Reformed confessions that were penned at the height of Calvin's influence between the years of 1559 and 1563. These confessions represented for Nevin the final stage in the development of Reformed doctrine and therefore presented the true doctrine of the Reformed Church on the Lord's Supper by providing a synthesis of the two diverging, but complementary, streams of sixteenth century Reformed thought on the issue. Nevin thus stood by his original presentation of this doctrine as well as his charge against the Reformed churches of the nineteenth century of apostasy from the same.

According to James Hastings Nichols, "Hodge did not reply. He was beyond his depth and, whether he fully realized it or not, he had been demolished."[85] Nichols is a sympathetic interpreter of Nevin, but scholars of all varieties who have looked at the historical features of this controversy share a similar opinion, though with varying degrees of enthusiasm.[86]

The differences between Hodge and Nevin on the question of the original Reformed doctrine of the Lord's Supper were conditioned primarily by their divergent approaches to the interpretation of history. Hodge was concerned—given his Baconian frame of mind—with compiling facts which corresponded to what may be seen as "self-evident" according to the dictates of common sense. This applied to the field of history no less than it did to other areas. Thus, Hodge tended to view the record of history as a "store-house of facts" no less than he did Scripture. John Williamson Nevin, on the other hand, as a moderate Hegelian, was wholeheartedly devoted to an organic theory of historical development, and he therefore sought to move beyond the citation of isolated historical proof-texts and toward an analysis of the underlying meaning behind the sources in question in light of the movement of history. Nevin understood well that history, and especially the history of ideas, does not exist in a sort of pristine vacuum. And so, when interpreting writings from an earlier age he saw it as necessary to first attempt to enter into the "life" of that age and to understand the thought-forms and meaning of terms in

85. Nichols, *Romanticism in American Theology*, 89

86. For example: Mathison, *Given for You*, 136–56; Holifield "Mercersburg, Princeton, and the South;" Hart, *John Williamson Nevin*, 123–37; Gerrish, *Tradition in the Modern World*, 60–70; Wallace "History and Sacrament."

use at the time in question, rather than isolating facts from each other, interpreting them according to modern modes of thought and speech, and proceeding to arrange them in whatever manner may suit one's purposes best.

On the Eucharistic theology of John Calvin in particular, Nevin demonstrated that he did have a much better grasp of the issues and relevant sources than Hodge had. However, this is not to say that Nevin's presentation of the overall history was faultless. It was in fact flawed at certain important points. For instance, although he was essentially correct in his interpretation and exposition of Calvin's sacramental theology, Nevin's contention that *all* the Reformed Confessions of the latter half of the sixteenth century ought to be interpreted in full conformity with Calvin's most comprehensive expositions of his own personal understanding of the Lord's Supper is somewhat problematic.[87] Further, Hodge was right to hold concerning the *Consensus Tigurinus*, against Nevin, that both Calvin and Bullinger had compromised in its formulation (even if he may not have been entirely accurate in his interpretation of that document). [88] And Hodge was also right to press both the diversity of opinion on the Eucharist among the Reformed in the first half of the sixteenth century as well as the variety of ways in which the doctrine came to be expressed in the Reformed Confessions. While Nevin did admit diversity to a degree, his emphasis on the organic development of history led him to stress a unity of thought

87. Richard Muller has effectively argued against such an approach to Reformation historiography in (among other places), "Calvin and the Calvinists, Part II," 134–38.

88. See footnote #68 of this chapter.

amongst the Reformed of the latter half of the sixteenth century to a point that was perhaps not entirely consistent with the historical record.[89]

Therefore, we may conclude that the respective historical presentations of Nevin and Hodge were both problematic due to the fact that they were each convinced that they were arguing for *the* "authentic" Reformed doctrine of the Eucharist. Hodge was certainly mistaken in his conviction that Nevin's Eucharistic theology did not have support in the writings of Calvin and a variety of the sixteenth century confessions (like the Belgic, Old Scots, Gallican, and the doctrinal standard of Nevin's own German Reformed denomination—the Heidelberg Catechism). But Nevin's historiography necessitated an authoritative unified synthesis (which he saw in Calvin) that may not have painted a completely accurate picture, either. While it is clear that all the later sixteenth century Reformed Confessions reject a "bare memorial" view of the Eucharist, and that they all at least allow for Calvin's doctrine of the Lord's Supper, it is not clear that they all *necessarily* rule out the symbolic parallelism of Charles Hodge while at the same time absolutely requiring Nevin's (and Calvin's) instrumentalism.

Hodge and Nevin, therefore, differed on what exactly constituted the "fully developed" Reformed doctrine of the Eucharist primarily because, in their reading of the sources, they were looking for different things. In this regard, Nevin was right in his contention that Hodge seems to have read his understanding of theological propriety into the historical record. Hodge did, in fact, have his own theory of historical development. But for him, the Church's historical

89. See also Wallace, "History and Sacrament," 183.

development is primarily a development of *doctrine*, not of *life*, as was the case with Nevin. Hodge's sense of development was determined by his standards of consistency, clarity, and "common sense." This comes out, for example, in his article, *The First and Second Adam*, which was written in response to Samuel Barid's realist anthropology. In that article, Hodge spells out his understanding of the development of Reformation theology:

> The truth is usually elicited by conflict; agreement is the result of comparison and adjustment of divergences. We accordingly find in the history of Protestant theology much more of inconsistency and confusion during the sixteenth than during the seventeenth century. It was not until one principle had been allowed to modify another, that the scheme of doctrine came to adjust itself to the consistent and moderate form in which it is presented in the writings of Turretin and Gerhard.[90]

Hence, Nevin and Hodge each tended to interpret the historical development of the Church in the same way that they understood the task of theology, and the Christian faith in general—Hodge emphasizing it as the development of a consistent system of doctrine, and Nevin emphasizing it as the historical unfolding of the life of Christ which is made progressively manifest in the unified confession of the Church.

However, while he was not without his own faults, Nevin was correct in his assessment that Hodge's histori-

90. "The First and the Second Adam," 90.

cal exposition was haphazard and on the whole shallow.[91] Nevin, for his part, in attempting to discover the genuine Reformed doctrine of the Holy Eucharist, did make a significant attempt to discern the flow of history, and he took appropriate notice of the *usus loquendi* of the period being analyzed. Charles Hodge, in many respects, did not. As a consequence, Hodge misinterpreted Calvin's doctrine of the Eucharist and, in turn, misunderstood and misrepresented Nevin's sacramental theology as something other than genuinely "Reformed." B. A. Gerrish has therefore correctly assessed the historical-theological presentation of the Princeton theologian's review of Nevin: "Hodge leaves us wondering whether it is possible to be both a Calvinist and a Presbyterian."[92]

Nevertheless, on this particular question Charles Hodge won the day in American Reformed Christianity. Nevin's sacramental views never took hold within the Reformed churches, while the doctrine of Hodge remains to this day the majority position of Reformed churches in the United States. In this vein, Keith Mathison's words ring quite true:

> [E]ven though Nevin won the historical battle, he lost the theological war. Hodge had the greater influence on his own generation, and

91. Nichols has stated concerning Hodge's historical argument: "Although he offered a pretentious parade of sources, all the important documentation, with one exception, he had borrowed without acknowledgment from *The Mystical Presence* in a fortnight or so, with no significant independent study, and to rearrange its historical evidence completely out of context in accordance with his own ideas of theological propriety" (*Romanticism in American Theology*, 90).

92. Gerrish, *Grace and Gratitude*, 5.

through the publication of his massive *Systematic Theology*, he extended his influence into future generations. Hodge's sacramental doctrine continues to have numerous adherents to this day, while few Reformed Christians have even heard of Nevin, and even fewer are aware of his debate with Hodge.[93]

93. Mathison, *Given for You*, 156.

3

Hubbub over a Hypostasis—
The Meaning of the Incarnation

THE CHRISTOLOGY
OF THE MYSTICAL PRESENCE

WHILE THE occasion for the controversy between Nevin and Hodge was their disagreement over the doctrine of the Reformed Church on the Lord's Supper, this was not the whole story. It was ultimately the topic of Christology which most pervasively conditioned how each theologian articulated his own particular version of Reformed Eucharistic theology. In this chapter we focus in on the Christological aspects of the Princeton-Mercersburg conflict.

The center of John W. Nevin's theological system is his conception of the mystical union between Christ and the Church through the incarnation. At the outset of *The Mystical Presence*, Nevin sets the tone for his treatment of this subject by providing a "free compressed translation" of an essay by Dr. Carl Ullmann (1796–1865), professor of theology at the University of Heidelberg, which was originally titled *The Distinctive Character of Christianity*, as a preliminary essay to his own work.[1] Ullmann's essay sets forth the idea—which was so fundamental for Nevin himself—that the nature of Christianity is essentially a *life*, rather than a set of doctrines or moral standards. This "life" spoken of by both Ullmann and Nevin is the divine-human life of Jesus Christ, whose incarnation forever retains its enduring force as the joining together of humanity with God in the one divine person of the eternal Logos. This fact in itself is the full realization of what mankind has always striven for—union with God. And herein lies the supremacy of Christianity far above all other religions which have ever existed: "Christianity is that religion which in the person of its author has actualized in fact, what all other religions have struggled in vain to reach, the unity of man with God."[2]

One may observe here the profound impact the thought patterns and categories of both Hegel and Schleirmacher as well as, more directly, the later mediating theologians (like Ullmann) had on Nevin's theology. As such, this is an appropriate place to address that influence a bit more fully than we had opportunity to do in chapter one.

The German influence on Nevin's thought was one of the largest reasons for the unpopularity of his theological program in a nineteenth century America that was thoroughly individualistic and had become enamored with the philosophy of "Common Sense."[3] This influence resulted in an intellectual gap between Nevin and the wider religious scene (and even the top theologians) of antebellum America

1. Nevin, *Mystical Presence*, 13–44.

2. Ibid., 42.

3. On the embrace of "common sense" reasoning by the majority of antebellum America see Noll, *America's God*, 229–38.

that left him open to profound misunderstanding by his critics. Most in his own day who would actually read what he wrote understood little of what he was saying or why he was saying it. Regarding this, Darryl G. Hart has commented concerning *The Mystical Presence*: "The German phrasing put off many of his Anglo-American critics, and it continues to create difficulty for those unfamiliar with the vicissitudes of nineteenth century German intellectual history."[4]

However, it is of vital importance to realize that Nevin was not merely a slavish follower of innovative German theologians.[5] Rather, he sought to assimilate what he saw as good and worthy in them with his own variety of Reformed confessionalism and his esteem for the teachings of the early church Fathers, particularly as those patristic beliefs found expression in the official creedal definitions of the early Church.

Nevin would in fact take pains, in a variety of publications, to distance himself from certain elements of the theology of both Scleiermacher and the mediating theologians. One particular instance of this may be seen in Nevin's "Answer" (1868) to the concerns of the man who was perhaps the most influential and important of all the mediating theologians, Isaak Dorner (1809–84). In that article, Nevin confessed that,

> We have been able to see and own thankfully the
> service which has been rendered to the cause of
> Christianity, through the intonation of this great

4. Hart, *John Williamson Nevin*, 123.

5. On this point, see Carlough, "German Idealism and the Theology of John W. Nevin," 40.

[Christological] principle, by Schleiermacher, and other master minds, who have followed him with far more orthodoxy than he ever had himself, without feeling ourselves bound in the least to accept in full all that any such master mind may have been led to deduce from the principle as belonging to the right construction of Christian doctrine. Our theology, in this view, has not been built upon Schleiermacher, or Ullmann, or Dorner, however much of obligation it cheerfully owes to each of them, as well as to others, whose more or less variant systems of thought go together to make up the conception of what is called the evangelical theology of Germany in its most modern form.[6]

Nevin then goes on to make it clear that it is historic, creedal, orthodox Christianity that is his ultimate authority: "Here it is that, with all our respect for German divinity, we consciously come to a break with it in our thoughts, and feel the necessity of supplementing it with the more practical ways of looking at Christianity which we find embodied in the ancient Creeds. *In this respect*, we freely admit, our theology is more Anglican than German. We stand upon the old Creeds. We believe in the Holy Catholic Church."[7]

6. Nevin, "Answer to Professor Dorner," 542.

7. Ibid., 542–43. Linden DeBie's comments on this subject are helpful. According to DeBie, the Mercersburg theologians, "replaced idealism's emphasis on the idea of Christ with the actual, historical person of Christ (as believed by orthodox tradition). The believer didn't so much rise into a higher level of God-consciousness made possible by Christ (as depicted in Schleiermacher's system), but became unified with the whole person of Christ. And their acceptance of the more Hebraic, material language of tradition, which endorsed

Regarding the theology of the *Mystical Presence*, specifically, even Ullmann's preliminary essay guards against
a complete adherence to Schleiermacher's theological system, saying that it "is found deficient through the want of a
proper appreciation of the nature of sin."[8] It was therefore
not at all Nevin's purpose to do away with the Reformation
doctrines of sin or atonement.[9] Much to the contrary, his
concern was to firmly establish the doctrine of the atonement by grounding it in the enduring reality of the *person*
of Christ. The incarnate Christ, according to Nevin, is
the only one who could ever accomplish the redemption
of man, precisely because he has brought humanity into
union with the divine nature in his very person. This is of
vital importance to keep in mind when interpreting Nevin's
continual statements about the importance and supremacy
of the incarnation as the foundation for Christianity. In his
thinking, the incarnation is not something to be thought
of as an isolated event, much less is it to be conceived apart
from the atonement for sins and the victory over death
wrought by Christ's crucifixion and resurrection. Rather,
the incarnation, as the entrance of God into humanity, *es-*

---

the ontological existence of evil and sin, was blatantly absent in both
Hegel and Schleiermacher" (*Speculative Theology and Common-Sense
Religion*, 68–69).

8. Nevin, *Mystical Presence*, 24.

9. Regarding the concern of the Mercersburg theologians to retain
a robust doctrine of sin, DeBie has commented that "mankind's
depravity was one Calvinist tenet they would not adjust. Sin and
miracles embarrassed rationalists, but they confused idealists.
Mercersburg would have its idealism wed to a supernaturalism that
preserved orthodoxy" (*Speculative Theology and Common-Sense
Religion*, 70).

tablishes the efficacy and enduring force of the atonement and thus also the entirety of Christian redemption.

Nevin begins his presentation of the incarnation in *The Mystical Presence*, then, by explaining that the world of mankind lay in universal ruin due to the sin of Adam and Eve. There is a real, organic connection between Adam and the rest of humanity, and it is on this basis that the Adamic guilt and corruption have become that of the entire race. To view this transfer of corruption as merely a formal imputation of guilt is to hold to a fundamentally Pelagian and individualistic conception of human nature, as Nevin sees it:

> The whole Pelagian view of life is shallow in the extreme. It sees in the human race only a vast aggregation of particular men, outwardly put together; a huge living sand-heap, and nothing more. But the human race is not a sand-heap. It is the power of a single life. It is bound together, not outwardly, but inwardly. Men have been one before they became many; and as many, they are still one. We have a perfect right then to say that Adam's sin is imputed to his posterity. Only let us not think of a mere outward transfer in the case. Against *such* imputation the objection commonly made to the doctrine has force. It would be to substitute a fiction for a fact. No imputation of that sort is taught in the Bible. But the imputation of Adam's sin to his posterity involves no fiction. It is counted to them simply because it is theirs in fact.[10]

10. Nevin, *Mystical Presence*, 155. The connection Nevin draws here between Adam's first sin and the corruption of the race is another key element of his thought that distinguishes it from the system of Schleiermacher. Schleiermacher held that no significant

Thus, due to the original sin and consequent corruption of the first man, mankind in general, because of its organic union with that first man, has been thrust into a state of helpless corruption, sin, and death.

However, because of the hypostatic union of humanity with the divine nature in Jesus Christ, who is truly the *Second Adam*, fallen humanity has been exalted again in him to a state of incorruption. Christ assumed, crucified, and raised up the entirety of human nature in his person. Such a conception of the union between Christ and humanity is, according to Nevin, the foundation for any lasting value in Christ's suffering, death, and resurrection. Christ's life is therefore given to his people in reality, not simply by way of outward imputation:

> The atonement as a foreign work, could not be
> made to reach us in the way of a true salvation.
> Only as it may be considered *immanent* in our

change took place within human nature on account of the first sin committed (and whether or not Adam and Eve were really historical figures was of little importance to him). For Schleiermacher, original sin is the tendency rooted deep within all men for the passion of the flesh—which was present within humanity even before the first sin was committed—to overcome and drown out the potential for God-consciousness. Christ therefore, according to Schleiermacher, came as the ideal man in order to restore this God-consciousness within humanity. (See Schleiermacher, *The Christian Faith*, 285–305.) Over against this, Nevin's articulation of the fall, sin, and redemption stands diametrically opposed. It is especially important to note two things specifically regarding Nevin's relation to Schleiermacher: 1. Nevin's guiding principle of the universal guilt and corruption of mankind due to the sin and corruption of the first man is absent in Schleiermacher, and 2. Schleiermacher's principles of the "feeling of absolute dependence" and "God-consciousness" do not condition Nevin's doctrine of redemption as they do Schleiermacher's.

> nature itself, can it be imputed to us as ours, and
> so become available in us for its own ends. And
> this is its character in truth. It holds in human-
> ity, as a work wrought out by it in Christ. When
> Christ died and rose, humanity died and rose at
> the same time in his person; just as it had fallen
> before in the person of Adam.[11]

Accordingly, it is not enough for Christ to have simply *done* for man what man could not *do* (that is, atone for sins committed) since this only deals with the guilt of sin. While such atonement for guilt is indeed necessary, it is even more fundamental that Christ *be* what humanity cannot *be*. Only in this way can the organic corruption which entered the race through the disobedience and corruption of the first parents be dealt with. Hence, in the incarnation Christ, by assuming human nature, united humanity with his divine nature and thereby elevated the race to a status which could not otherwise have been achieved:

> That the race might be saved, it was necessary that
> a work should be wrought not beyond it, but in
> it; and this inward salvation to be effective must
> lay hold of the race itself in its organic, universal
> character, before it could extend to individuals,
> since in no other form was it possible for it to
> cover fully the breadth and depth of the ruin that
> lay in its way. Such an inward salvation of the
> race required that it should be joined in a living
> way with the divine nature itself, as represented
> by the everlasting Word or *Logos*, the fountain of
> all created light and life. The Word accordingly

11. Nevin, *Mystical Presence*, 157.

became flesh, that is assumed humanity into
union with itself.[12]

Flowing from Nevin's understanding of the organic
union between Christ and humanity is his perspective on
the believer's mystical union with Christ. According to
Nevin, salvation is an existential fact of the Christian's life.
The very power of Jesus Christ's resurrected life is actually
communicated to the being of the believer in a dynamic
way: "Christ communicates his own life substantially to the
soul on which he acts, causing it to grow into his very nature. This is the *mystical union*; the basis of our whole salvation; the only medium by which it is possible for us to have
an interest in the grace of Christ under any other view."[13]
Therefore Christ, the ideal man, communicates his own life
to his people, activating within them a divine power which
renews their corrupted nature, eventually culminating in
the eschatological resurrection.[14] This understanding of the
mystical union between Christ and believers bears some
similarities to the vine and branches analogy employed by
Jesus in the narrative of John's Gospel (15. 1–6), and this is
used by Nevin as support for his doctrine.[15]

Christianity then, according to Nevin, is in essence a
new life, not merely a set of doctrines or moral standards.
The divine-human life of Christ—the fountainhead of the
Christian faith—is communicated to his people through
the work of the Holy Ghost, thus constituting the Christian

12. Ibid., 156.
13. Ibid., 159.
14. Ibid., 166.
15. Ibid., 216.

Church. Believers consequently share one life with Christ by virtue of their mystical union with him by the Spirit, and this life, being thus made truly theirs, is the foundation of their redemption.

Because of the emphasis he placed on the hypostatic union of the divine and human natures of Christ in his thought, Nevin was led to challenge the doctrines of the atonement and imputation as they were understood in his day by the majority of conservative Protestants. For Nevin, Jesus is not just the federal representative of His people; he actually takes up the nature of his people and communicates his nature to them. This brought him into opposition with those theologians—like Charles Hodge—who held that it was Christ's work of atonement that was most crucial and that, consequently, the incarnation was brought about primarily so that Jesus could pay the penalty for the guilt of sins and that his righteousness could be imputed in a forensic way to his people as their representative. This way of looking at redemption was unthinkable for Nevin, because it does not deal with what he saw as humanity's most fundamental problem: the organic corruption of human nature brought about through the fall of Adam.

Nevertheless, it should also be noted that, although he does relegate the atonement to a secondary status below the incarnation in his system, Nevin does not do away completely with its significance, for he declares the atonement to have been completely necessary for the forgiveness of sins.[16] But he is clear that the atonement is only effica-

---

16. Ibid., 157. In an 1870 article from the *Mercersburg Review*, entitled "Once for All," Nevin would write: "The whole Gospel centres in the death of Christ. Here, in a profound sense, we have the ground

cious to redeem mankind as it relates to the union of the divine nature with humanity in Christ's person. Also, Nevin denies a strictly forensic understanding of the atonement because, according to him, sin is a deeply rooted organic fact of human existence and must be dealt with within our nature, rather than outside of it. As Nevin sees it, all the legal imputation of righteousness in the world will avail for nothing if human nature itself is not elevated from its state of corruption: "The atonement as a foreign work, could not be made to reach us in the way of a true salvation. Only as it may be considered *immanent* in our nature itself, can it be imputed to us as ours, and so become available in us for its own ends . . . When Christ died and rose, humanity died and rose at the same time in his person: not figuratively, but truly; just as it had fallen before in the person of Adam."[17]

However, Nevin does not deny forensic imputation as such. In fact, he claims that placing the atonement under the incarnation in order of importance actually establishes the doctrine of imputation:

> Do we then discard the doctrine of imputation,
> as maintained by the orthodox theology in op-
> position to the vain talk of the Pelagians? By no
> means. We seek only to *establish* the doctrine; for
> without it, most assuredly, the whole structure of
> Christianity must give way. It is only when placed

---

of our redemption; because here only we have the atonement—the sacrifice which takes away sin, and through this the victory, at the same time, which makes room for life and immortality" (100). And later in the same article he goes on to say that the atonement for sins in the death of Christ "is the only and whole ground of our justification before God" (103).

17. Nevin, *Mystical Presence*, 157.

on false ground that it becomes untenable in the
way now stated . . . The Bible knows nothing of a
simply outward imputation, by which something
is reckoned to a man that does not belong to him
in fact . . . The scriptures make two cases, in this
respect, fully parallel. We are justified freely by
God, on the ground of what Christ has done and
suffered in our room and stead. His righteousness is imputed to us, set over to our account,
regarded as our own. But here again the relation
in *law*, supposes and shows a corresponding relation in *life*. The forensic declaration by which the
sinner is pronounced free from guilt, is like that
word in the beginning when God said *let there
be light*, and light was. It not only proclaims him
righteous for Christ's sake, but sets the righteousness of Christ in him as part of his own life.[18]

Thus, the doctrine of the imputation of Christ's righteousness does have a place in Nevin's system, but not in the
way he considered it to have been taught by most Reformed
theologians of his own day. For Nevin, the imputation of
Christ's righteousness necessarily carries with it also the
impartation of Christ's life. These two sides of redemption
must be distinguished, but they cannot be separated.[19]

18. Ibid., 180.

19. Calvin had written, in response to Osiander, in *Institutes*
3.11.10, "I confess that we are deprived of this utterly incomparable
good [justification] until Christ is made ours. Therefore, that joining
together of head and members, that indwelling of Christ in our
hearts--in short, that mystical union—are accorded by us the highest
degree of importance, so that Christ, having been made ours, makes
us sharers with him in the gifts with which he has been endowed.
We do not, therefore, contemplate him outside ourselves from afar in

As he brings *The Mystical Presence* to a conclusion, Nevin seeks to offer a biblical defense of his doctrine.[20] It is his highest concern in this section to give Scriptural support for his understanding of the incarnation and the mystical union, since these form the foundation of his entire theological system. The prologue of John's Gospel provides Nevin with his primary argument for the centrality of the incarnation in redemption.[21] With regard to his understanding of the union between Christ and humanity, the Pauline doctrine of the first and second Adam contained in Romans 5:12–21 and 1 Corinthians 15:21–22, 45–49 is the principal support offered. Christ, according to Nevin, did not just become a particular man, but he became *flesh*, that is, "humanity in its universal conception."[22]

Nevin also provides an abundance of biblical support for his conception of Christianity as a life rather than a set of doctrines from various passages in both the Johannine and Pauline writings.[23] He goes on to offer an analysis of

---

order that his righteousness may be imputed to us, but because we put on Christ and are engrafted into his body–in short, because he deigns to make us one with him. For this reason, we glory that we have fellowship of righteousness with him." On Calvin's doctrine of union with Christ and its relation to both the forensic and renovative aspects of redemption, see Garcia, *Life in Christ*, and Evans, *Imputation and Impartation*, 6–68.

20. The fact that this biblical defense comes so late in the work betrays Nevin's traditionalist frame of mind. He believed it to be of utmost importance for a proper interpretation of Scripture to view it first from a correct theological perspective derived from the interpretations and traditions of the Church through history.

21. Nevin, *Mystical Presence*, 187–92.

22. Ibid., 197.

23. Ibid., 200–207. Passages cited in this section are: John 14:9,

John 6:51–58 and to defend various other aspects of his Eucharistic doctrine. But the most important areas of his biblical treatment have to do with his defense of mystical union with Christ and of Christianity as a life, as these are the foundational features of his theology.

As we have already pointed out in chapter two, Nevin viewed Scripture as an organic whole, the contents of which could only be properly interpreted by one who already possesses a comprehensive—or "catholic" or "organic"—theological perspective. To Nevin's mind, a theological argument does not stand or fall with the collection and citation of various proof-texts. Even though he did attempt to provide them, Nevin's compilation of texts seems almost like an after-thought, perhaps begrudgingly assembled in anticipation of the criticisms that were bound to come his way to the effect that he was not concerned with the teachings of Scripture.

To be sure, Nevin did believe his doctrine to be fully in line with Scripture. But the method by which he arrived at his conclusions was wholly different from the methodology employed by most other nineteenth century American evangelical theologians. Nevin considered it essential that, before attempting to exegete particular passages of Scripture, one embrace a theological system in line with a comprehensive understanding of Scripture as a whole, which system Nevin considered to be presented—at least in

---

14:6, 5:11–12, 5:24–26, 11:25—26; 1 Cor. 15:21–23; Rom. 8:29; Col. 1:17–20; Heb. 1:2; Eph. 1:22—2:31 Cor. 1:24, 30; 2 Cor. 1:20, 5:4–6; Gal. 3:27–28, 5:15; Eph. 2:13–22, 5:14–16; Col. 1:20, 3:10–11; Gal. 2:20; Eph. 1:18—23, 2:1–10; Phil. 3:7–11; Col. 3:3–4.

seed form—in the Apostles' Creed.[24] Only then may individual passages be properly interpreted, as informed by the
entirety of Scripture and guided by the historic interpretations of the Church:

> A theology that builds all its doctrines upon
> mere abstract texts, may arrogate to itself the
> character of *biblical*, in the most eminent sense;
> but it can never have any good claim to be so in
> reality. It belongs to the very genius of *sect*, to
> magnify itself in this way. It always affects to be
> biblical, in the highest degree. It will stand upon
> the bible, and upon nothing but the bible. In
> the end however, its biblicity is found to resolve
> itself invariably into such a poor, circumscribed
> conception of revealed truth, as is not described.
> Isolated texts, viewed through the medium of
> some particular sect hobby, are made to exhaust
> the whole proof, whether for or against the posi-
> tion on which they are made to bear. But no use
> of the scriptures can well be more truly unbibli-
> cal than this. Christianity is not a skeleton, nor

24. The esteem in which Nevin held the historic creeds, and
particularly the Apostles' Creed, is important to keep in mind
with regard to his exegesis. Although he does not offer any detailed
discussion of this in the *Mystical Presence*, Nevin makes it clear in
numerous other places that he saw the historic Creeds as normative
for a proper interpretation of Scripture. The ancient Creeds set forth
the order of doctrines and the organic structure in which the Christian
theologian is to stand in order to properly interpret Scripture. This
comes out most fully throughout Nevin's four articles on the "Apostle's
Creed," in volume I of the *Mercersburg Review* (1849). He states in the
third article of this series, on the *Material Structure or Organism* of the
Creed, that "all true theology . . . grows forth from the Creed, and so
remains bound to it perpetually as its necessary radix or root" (341).

> yet a corpse for the use of the dissecting room . . .
> All turns on the position of the beholder himself,
> and his power of observing and comprehending
> the revelation as a whole . . . All turns on the
> stand-point of the interpreter, and the compre-
> hensive catholicity of his view.[25]

Nevin could have said few things toward the conclusion of his work that would have cut against the grain of
what Charles Hodge viewed as the task of a theologian
more than this.

HODGE'S CRITIQUE

Despite his numerous attempts to clarify that he was
seeking to recover the original Reformed teaching on the
church and the sacraments and to safeguard the Protestant
doctrines of the atonement and imputation against abstraction, many Protestant theologians took exception to Nevin's
theology on precisely these points. As Maxwell has put it,
"So theologically encompassing was Nevin's view of the

---

25. Nevin, *Mystical Presence*, 230–31. Nevin would strike a similar
chord later when reviewing Charles Hodge's commentary on St. Paul's
epistle to the Ephesians: "[T]he theological scheme with which an
interpreter comes to the exposition of the Bible, is more deserving
of consideration than any isolated truths of his exegetical learning
aside from this. Our theology, or want of theology, must always rule
our exegesis. The notion of a purely grammatical exegesis, as urged
by the school of Ernesti, is simply absurd. No amount of philological
or historical learning can of itself lead to a trustworthy exposition
of what the Scriptures actually say and teach. The case requires, in
addition to this, an inward correspondence and sympathy of mind
on the part of the expositor, with the world of truth he is called to
expound" ("Hodge on the Ephesians, article 1," 48).

incarnation that he understood the atonement only in light of it, and this seeming deprecation brought him not a few critics."[26] Charles Hodge was, if not the most persistent or militant, certainly the most recognizable of these critics. Hodge did not only take exception to particular doctrines, but rather attacked Nevin's entire theological system at its foundations. From there he proceeded to draw all kinds of conclusions about the logical consequences of Nevin's thought, proceeding with the conviction that if the root is bad, the tree will bear nothing but bad fruit.

Thus, after offering his review of Nevin's exposition of the Reformed doctrine of the Eucharist in his article *The Doctrine of the Reformed Church on the Lord's Supper*, Charles Hodge proceeded to provide a summary and criticism of the overall theory on which Nevin built his theological system. From the outset Hodge confessed the difficulty he had in attempting to understand Nevin's theology: "It is not an easy thing to give a just and clear exhibition of a theory confessedly mystical, and which involves some of the most abstruse points both of anthropology and theology."[27] Nevertheless, he does provide an adequate and fair, though somewhat hurried and incomplete, summary of the fundamental features of Nevin's anthropology and the implications drawn from it to the areas of Christology and soteriology.[28] After laying out his understanding of Nevin's theological system, however, Hodge claims that, "It is in all its essential features Schleiermacher's theory."[29]

26. Maxwell, *Worship and Reformed Theology*, 27.

27. Hodge, *Essays and Reviews*, 373.

28. Ibid., 374–78

29. Ibid., 378.

Hodge then states that he does not intend to examine the truth of Nevin's theology, but only its relation to the Reformed tradition as well as the universal convictions of the historic Church catholic: "We propose very briefly to assign our reasons for regarding his system . . . as an entire rejection not only of the peculiar doctrines of the Reformed church on the points concerned, but of some of the leading principles of Protestant, and even Catholic, theology."[30]

Hodge's first criticism of Nevin's theory is that it is "very plain" that Nevin's doctrine of the incarnation and hypostatic union is "a departure not only from the doctrine of the Reformed church, but of the church universal." It is, according to Hodge, in essence the same thing as both the Eutychian and Monothelite heresies: "Substitute the word life, for its equivalent, nature, and we have the precise statement of Dr. Nevin's." Hodge therefore claims that Nevin agrees with these heresies, and comes out against the orthodox creedal definition of the person of Christ, because in Nevin's theory Christ possesses one φυσις and one ενεργεια. However, he does not provide any citations from Nevin that necessitate reading his use of "life" as being in some sense equivalent to the terms φυσις or ενεργεια as they were understood in the context of the fifth-century Christological controversies. Rather, he simply assumes that Nevin has something similar to these terms in mind whenever he speaks of "life."[31] His only support for this

30. Ibid., 378.

31. Ibid., 379. It should be noted that Nevin himself does not imply such a connection in *The Mystical Presence*, and the current writer has not been able to find an explicit equation of *life* with *nature* or *essence* in any of his writings.

understanding of Nevin is an appeal to Schleiermacher's theology: "We are confirmed in the correctness of this view of the matter, from the fact, that Schleiermacher, the father of this system, strenuously objects to the use of the word *nature* in this whole connection especially in its application to the divinity, and opposes also the adoption of the terms which the council of Chalcedon employed in the condemnation of Eutychianism."[32] Thus, again, Hodge betrays his tendency to equate Nevin with Schleiermacher.

Hodge further charges Nevin with departure from the catholic tradition on the incarnation because Nevin had pointed out certain problems in the psychology of Calvin. He claims that this in itself is enough to indict Nevin with heterodoxy in his formulation of the person of Christ: "No one, however, has ever pretended that Calvin had any peculiar views on that subject. He says himself that he held all the decisions, as to such points, of the first six ecumenical councils. In differing from Calvin, on this point, therefore, Dr. Nevin differs from the whole church."[33]

After this, Hodge charges Nevin's theory with necessarily tending both towards a denial of the full deity of Christ as well as pantheism, because of his description of Christ as the "ideal man":

> But is a perfect, or ideal man, anything more than a mere man after all? If all that was in Christ pertains to the perfection of our nature, he was, at best, but a perfect man. The only way to escape Socinianism, on this theory, is by deifying man, identifying the divine and human, and

32. Ibid., 379.
33. Ibid.

making all the glory, wisdom, and power, which belong to Christ, the proper attitudes of humanity. Christ is a perfect man. But what is a perfect man? We may give a pantheistic, or a Socinian answer to that question, and not really help the matter—for the real and infinite hiatus between us and Christ, is in either case closed . . . We of course do not attribute to Dr. Nevin either of these forms of doctrine. We do not believe that he adopts either, but we object both to his language and doctrine that one or the other of those heresies is their legitimate consequence.[34]

Hodge then proceeds to charge Nevin with deviation from the Reformed as well as the universal Church in his doctrine of union with Christ. Hodge accepts the idea, propounded by Nevin, that union with Christ is "not merely moral, nor is it merely legal or federal, nor does it arise simply from Christ having assumed our nature," but is rather "at the same time real and vital" between the believer and Christ himself.[35] However, he considers it the orthodox doctrine that the Holy Spirit alone unites believers with Christ, and that it is by receiving the Spirit that we receive Christ along with his life. Hodge even allows for a special power emanating from the glorified body of Christ in heaven to the believer, but states that even this "falls very far short, or

34. Ibid., 380. The language of Christ as the ideal or perfect man is, however, not unique to either Nevin or Schleiermacher. It has ample patristic support. See, for one example, the epistle of St. Ignatius to the Smyrneans, 4.2. Also, the Definition of Chalcedon confesses that Christ is "perfect in manhood" (τελειον . . . εν ανθρωποτητι).

35. Hodge, *Essays and Reviews*, 380.

rather is something entirely different from the doctrine of this book."[36]

The theory of Nevin, Hodge writes, "is determined by his view of the constitution of Christ's person." He then states Nevin's understanding of union with Christ thus: "Believers, therefore, receive, or take part in the entire humanity of Christ. From Adam they receive humanity as he had it, after the fall; from Christ, the theanthropic life, humanity with deity enshrined in it, or rather made one with it, one undivided life."[37] The problem here is that, as Hodge sees it, Nevin's theory obliterates the role of the Holy Spirit in the union of believers with Christ,[38] and is therefore a deviation from the orthodox Christian faith and identical to the theology of Schleiermacher.

Hodge also objects that Nevin's understanding of union with Christ, as it hinges upon the incarnation, renders the mystical union different after the incarnation than what the Old Testament saints would have enjoyed before it. This, according to Hodge, is opposed to the majority Reformed view of the continuity of the people of God under the old and new dispensations. As he perceives the matter, the Reformed churches have always held that the spiritual experience of believers before and after Christ is essentially the same in everything other than in covenant administration and the degree of revelation given.[39] He

36. Ibid., 381.

37. Ibid.

38. However, Nevin had been very careful to explicitly state that the entire union is effected by the Holy Spirit. See, for example, *Mystical Presence*, 51, 57.

39. Hodge, *Essays and Reviews*, 381–82.

provides some relevant passages from Calvin to show the difference between the Reformer of Geneva and Nevin on this point, after which he asserts that "The lowest Puritan, ultra Protestant, or sectary in the land, who truly believes in Christ, is nearer Calvin than Dr. Nevin; and has more of the true spirit and theology of the Reformed church, than is to be found in this book."[40]

Thereafter Hodge points out how Nevin's teaching concerning the person of Christ and the mystical union affects his presentation of Christ's work: "Dr. Nevin's theory, differing so seriously from that of the Reformed church, as to the person of Christ and his union with his people, may be expected to differ from it as to the nature of Christ's work, and the method of salvation."[41] Here he takes issue

40. Ibid., 383. While Hodge's criticism of Nevin on this point holds some weight, he oversimplifies Calvin's presentation of the matter. Although Calvin certainly taught that Old Covenant believers enjoyed the same spiritual *benefits* as New Covenant believers, the incarnation nevertheless retained a central role in his conception of the communication of these benefits under both dispensations. Calvin in fact held that there is a difference in the manner in which the people of God receive Christ under the administration of the New Covenant as opposed to that of the Old Covenant. This comes out explicitly in his commentary on 1 Corinthians 10:3–4, where he states that the reception of Christ by the people of God under the old dispensation was "by the secret work of the Holy Spirit, who wrought in them in such a manner, that Christ's flesh, though not yet created, was made efficacious in them. He means, however, that they ate in their own way, *which was different from ours*, and . . . that Christ is now presented to us more fully, according to the revelation. For, in the present day, *the eating is substantial, which it could not have been then*—that is, Christ feeds us with his flesh, which has been sacrificed for us, and appointed as our food, and from this we derive life" (*Calvin's Commentaries, Vol. XX*, 320. Emphasis mine).

41. Hodge, *Essays and Reviews*, 384.

with Nevin's contention that the incarnation, rather than the atonement, is the foundation of man's redemption. The biggest sticking point for Hodge on this score is Nevin's lack of emphasis on a *substitutionary* atonement, specifically:

> What however are we to say to this view of the atonement? It was vicarious suffering indeed . . . But there is here no atonement, that is, no satisfaction; no propitiation of God; no reference to divine justice. All this is necessarily excluded. All these ideas are passed over in silence by Dr. Nevin; by Schleiermacher they are openly rejected. The atonement is the painfully accomplished triumph of the new divine principle introduced into our nature, over the law of sin introduced into it by the sin of Adam. Is this the doctrine of the Reformed church?[42]

Hodge follows this analysis by offering a string of citations from *The Mystical Presence* which demonstrate that the foundation of redemption in Nevin's system is in fact the incarnation. However, the statements made by Nevin concerning the necessity of atonement as well as his qualifications to the effect that he was seeking to root imputation in the more foundational (in Nevin's view) doctrine of mystical union with Christ are simply glossed over.

It is clear that the doctrines of atonement and imputation, as far as Hodge was concerned, were the main issues which superseded all others. Any theological system that would downplay the importance of the atonement and of forensic imputation by the divine declaration of justifica-

---

42. Ibid., 384.

tion—even if the one propounding it professed to hold to these doctrines—was completely unacceptable to him:

> Here we reach the very life-spot of the Reformation. Is justification a declaring just, or a making just, inherently? This was the real battle-ground on which the blood of so many martyrs was spilt. Are we justified for something done for us, or something wrought in us, actually our own? It is a mere playing with words to make a distinction . . . between what it is that thus makes us inherently righteous. Whether it is infused grace, a new heart, the indwelling Spirit, the humanity of Christ, his life, his theanthropic nature; it is all one. It is subjective justification after all, and nothing more. We consider Dr. Nevin's doctrine as impugning here, the vital doctrine of Protestantism. His doctrine is not, of course, the Romish, *teres atque rotundus*; he may distinguish here, and discriminate there. But as to the main point, it is a denial of the Protestant doctrine of justification.[43]

Thus, the main issue for the original Protestants, without exception, was that a foreign righteousness which is not our own is imputed to us, and it is precisely this doctrine that, according to Hodge, is denied by Nevin.[44]

43. Ibid., 385–86.

44. For his part, Nevin never denies that this was in fact the main issue for the Reformers in their disputes with the Roman Catholic Church over the doctrine of justification. Rather, he contends that they did not leave the doctrine of justification wholly in the abstract. Nevin holds that forensic justification is made a reality to man through a mystical life-union with the incarnate, resurrected Christ. Here, Hodge can talk about a real living union with Christ all he

Hodge then brings his criticism of Nevin's theory back to his doctrine of the church and the sacraments. He states that Nevin rejects the evangelical understanding, as propounded by Luther and Calvin, that one comes to faith in Christ and then on this basis enters into the church, rather than coming to Christ through the church: "The main question whether we come to Christ and then to the church; whether we by a personal act of faith receive him, and by union with him become a member of his mystical body; or whether all our access to Christ is through a mediating church, Dr. Nevin decides against the evangelical system."[45]

To Nevin's statement that "An outward church is the necessary form of the new creation in Christ Jesus, in its very nature," Hodge counters that, "It would be difficult to frame a proposition more subversive to the very foundations of all Protestantism . . . It is the fundamental error of Romanism, the source of her power and of her corruption, to ascribe to the outward church the attributes and prerogatives of the mystical body of Christ."[46] Hodge also objects to Nevin's contention that the sacraments convey a unique grace which has an objective efficacy, claiming that his opinion on this matter is "somewhere between the Romish and Lutheran view."[47]

---

wants, but for Nevin, if no connection is drawn between imputation and this union, all would seem to be empty words.

45. Hodge, *Essays and Reviews*, 387.

46. Ibid., 387.

47. Ibid., 388. This charge is nearly astounding given Nevin's continual rejection in *The Mystical Presence* of any local presence of Christ in the elements as well as any hint of a *manducatio impiorum*, and his repeated assertions concerning the communication of Christ

Hodge concludes his criticism of *The Mystical Presence* by claiming that Nevin's system is "only a specious form of Rationalism... in its essential element a psychology."[48] He decries Nevin's view as wholly subjective, stating that in his theology, "the only Christ we have or need, is an inward principle," which does away with the objective, historical Christ. Hodge further charges Nevin with Sabellianism, because of his contention that Christ is present along with the Spirit.[49] He interprets Nevin as teaching that, "The Spirit is . . . not the third person of the Trinity, but the thean-thropic nature of Christ as it dwells in the church. We do not suppose that Dr. Nevin has consciously discarded the doctrine of the Trinity; but we fear that he has adopted a theory which destroys that doctrine."[50]

Finally, to conclude his scathing review, Hodge tells us that he had written his harsh polemic with regret:

---

to the believer by the Spirit, received through faith.

48. Ibid., 389.

49. Ibid., 390–91. Nevin had argued in *The Mystical Presence* that "The persons of the adorable Trinity are indeed distinct. But we must beware of sundering them into abstract subsistences, one without the other. They subsist in the way of most perfect mutual inbeing and intercommunication. The Spirit of Christ is not his representative or surrogate simply, as some would seem to think; but Christ himself under a certain mode of subsistence" (212). Here, Hodge seems to neglect the qualifications that Nevin places on his presentation of this topic and focuses completely on the last clause. However, if Nevin is read charitably and with due heed taken to his clearly stated qualifications, he need not be interpreted as advocating anything other than the patristic doctrine of *perichoresis*, or the mutual indwelling and interpenetration of the Trinitarian persons.

50. Hodge, *Essays and Reviews*, 391.

We said at the commencement of this article, that we had never read Dr. Nevin's book on the Mystical Presence, until now. We have from time to time read other of his publications, and looked here and there into the work before us; and have thus been led to fear that he was allowing the German modes of thinking to get the mastery over him, but we had no idea that he had so far given himself up to their influence. If he has any faith in friendship and long continued regard, he must believe that we could not find ourselves separated from him by such serious differences, without deep regret, and will therefore give us credit for sincerity of conviction and purpose.[51]

NEVIN'S RESPONSE

Charles Hodge's various criticisms of John Nevin's theological system left little doubt that he considered his former student to be "of a different spirit" from Protestant orthodoxy, and even from catholic orthodoxy generally. By the end of his review of *The Mystical Presence*, Hodge had come to impugn Nevin's system for being nearly identical to, or at least tending toward, no less than eight different heterodox views at one point or another: 1. Schleiermacherian mysticism, 2. Rationalism, 3. Pantheism, 4. Socinianism, 5. Eutychianism, 6. Mothelitism, 7. Romanism, and 8.

51. The concluding paragraph is not contained in the edition of the review reprinted in *Essays and Reviews*. It may be found in the original article, published in the 1848 volume of *The Biblical Repertory and Princeton Review*, 278.

Sabellianism.[52] It mattered little to Hodge that some of these categories are mutually exclusive or that one man could not possibly have held to them all while remaining consistent with himself. Yet, that may very well have been Hodge's point, though it is not explicitly stated. He interpreted Nevin's theology in the same manner that he interpreted the theology of Schleiermacher as well as all other nineteenth century German theologians—a mass of utter confusion and inconsistency.

It did not take long for Nevin to respond to Hodge's critique of the Christological features of his thought. In his work, *Antichrist, or the Spirit of Sect and Schism*, published in the same year that Hodge's review of *The Mystical Presence* appeared in the *Biblical Repertory and Princeton Review* (1848), Nevin undertook, in the form of a somewhat lengthy preface to that work, a defense of his theological system in light of Hodge's criticisms. Though not nearly as large as his historical response on the Reformed doctrine of the Lord's Supper, Nevin's preface to *Antichrist* does address most of the substantial Christological points raised by Hodge in his review.

It might be assumed, based on his preface the work, that the entirety of Nevin's polemic in *Antichrist* had the theology of Princeton specifically in its sights. However, while some of the ideas propounded by the Princeton theology were no doubt in view in many sections of Nevin's scathing criticism of what he calls "the spirit of sect and schism," the entire tract was not written with Hodge's review expressly

52. In light of this onslaught of accusations, B. A. Gerrish seems justified in his assessment that Hodge employed an "essentially hostile hermeneutic" of Nevin. (See his *Tradition in the Modern World*, 62.)

in mind. Nevin states at the very beginning of the preface that "the following tract has been partially presented, in three different places, during the course of the past year, from the pulpit . . . It is now issued accordingly, with new and more complete preparation, in its present form."[53] Hodge's review was published in 1848, and *Antichrist* was published in the same year. So, if Nevin is being truthful in his claim that the pamphlet is largely taken from sermons he had preached throughout the previous year, the entire work cannot have been intended as an answer to Hodge's review of *The Mystical Presence*. Also, Nevin's second paragraph implies that his answer to Hodge is confined to the preface, which was included only after the main body of the tract had been completed: "A review of my work on 'The Mystical Presence,' which has appeared in the last number of the 'Princeton Biblical Repertory,' attributed to the pen of Dr. Hodge, makes it proper for me to say a word here of my relation to Schleiermacher; with whose whole system that article has found it convenient to invest me, in the way of borrowed drapery, for the purpose of bringing my theology into discredit."[54]

Thus, Nevin's direct response to Hodge's criticisms of his theological system is contained in the preface of *Antichrist*, and he rightly frames this defense in the form of a clarification concerning his relation to Friedrich Schleiermacher. He begins by writing that although he had read some of Schleiermacher's works, and considered him a genius, he was nevertheless "not aware at all of having taken him, in any sense slavishly, for my master and guide." Nevin

53. Nevin, *Antichrist*, 3.
54. Ibid., 3.

was of course indebted to many theologians, both English and German, and Schleiermacher was one of them. "So," he says, "no doubt, I owe much to Schleiermacher. But it is simply in the way, in which all the evangelical thinking in Germany, at this time, is, more or less, impregnated with the deep suggestive power of his thoughts."[55]

But even though he admired Schleiermacher and considered him a genius, Nevin makes it clear that he believes Schleiermacher's system to be unorthodox and that it "ran out . . . into gross and dangerous errors." Nevertheless, Nevin cautions against throwing the baby out with the bathwater: "Does it follow still, however, that all his thinking was for this reason false, or that no part of it can be turned to account in such a way as to leave his errors behind? Princeton, I would say respectfully, has been too apt to deal in this sort of logic."[56]

His cautious reverence for the memory and genius of Schleiermacher thus stated, Nevin then points out that the real issue between him and Hodge, as he sees it, is the central place which the person of Christ, the significance of the incarnation, and the mystical union occupy in his thought. Nevin maintains that here he is not following Schleiermacher as much as he is following the orthodox Christological dogma of the ancient Creeds:

> But surely it is not necessary that either of these ideas should remain bound to the Rationalism and Sabellianism, which are charged by Dr. Hodge on the theory of Schleiermacher himself. To my mind at least, they fall in much more

55. Ibid., 3.
56. Ibid., 4.

easily with the full doctrine of the Athanasian creed; and it is in this form generally, if not universally, that they come into view, in what may now be called the reigning evangelical theology of Germany.[57]

He then claims that the statements made in Ulmann's essay—which was entirely endorsed by Nevin and added as a preface to *The Mystical Presence*—should have been enough to make it clear that his system was decidedly opposed to that of Scheleiermacher on some vital points.[58] Since Ulmann himself comes out against Scheleiermacher on the doctrines of sin and the atonement, and since Nevin endorses Ulmann's essay as providing an adequate summary of his own thinking on these points, Hodge should have, Nevin thinks, at least given him the benefit of the doubt that he was not simply regurgitating what he had read in Schleiermacher. He continues on to point out that, on top of Ullmann's preliminary essay, Nevin himself had made a significant effort to guard against misunderstanding on precisely these points:

> Besides fortifying myself here with the preliminary essay, borrowed from Ulmann, I had taken all proper pains, as I thought, in the body of my work itself, to show that I stood in no fellowship, either with the errors of Schleiermacher on the one hand, or with Hegel on the other. I have been somewhat surprised, I confess, that in spite of all these precautions, I am set down by Dr. Hodge as a simple borrower of some 'cast-off clothes'

57. Ibid., 5.
58. Ibid.

of the first, with a rag here and there perhaps from the second, just as though no such care had been taken to prevent this very wrong. The only natural construction to be put on this is, that Dr. Hodge holds me incapable of seeing clearly to what issue my system necessarily runs, and feels himself authorized accordingly to load it with all these as he has them clearly in his own mind.[59]

Having thus rejected the charge that he was of one mind with Schleiermacher and having also demonstrated that he had taken the necessary precautions which ought to have shielded him against such a charge, Nevin moves on to address some of the specific points raised by Hodge against his Christology. He begins by insisting again that, far from being open to the charge of the heresies toward which Schleiermacher tended, his conception of the centrality of Christ's person in the redemption of mankind comes primarily from the ancient church, and is therefore not necessarily tied in any way to Schleiermacher's unorthodox theology. Nevin asks, "Can any one see, how this should remain necessarily wedded to Schleiermacher's defective doctrine of the Trinity; and not rather acquire its highest force, when associated . . . with the ancient faith of the church?"[60]

Thus, Nevin once more makes it clear that he is not merely restating Schleiermacher's opinions, nor is he meaning to deny the Protestant doctrines of justification and imputation. Rather, he is attempting to take the Christological dogmas of the ancient Creeds and place them at the cen-

59. Ibid., 6.
60. Ibid., 7

ter of a theological system framed in nineteenth-century German thought forms (Nevin did after all teach at the seminary of the *German* Reformed church) while remaining within the general doctrinal guidelines provided by the sixteenth century Reformed Confessions (primarily the Heidelberg Catechism). He accordingly states concerning his Christology that, "It rejects neither the doctrine of Christ nor his work, but simply resolves their *value* into the constitution of his life."[61]

Next on Nevin's agenda is Hodge's charge of pantheism. He claims here that his emphasis on the union of the divine nature with human nature in Christ's person, far from being open to the charge of pantheism, is nothing other than historic, orthodox Christian teaching on the incarnation. Hence, to Hodge's indictment of pantheism, Nevin thrusts back at him the charge of denying the true meaning of Christ's incarnation:

> Either the supernatural entered into organic, that is, real and historical union, with the natural, in the person of Christ, or we must say of the whole mystery, that it was an optical illusion simply, or at most a passing theophany in the style of the Old Testament. The difference between such a theophany and a real incarnation, does not depend certainly on the measure of mere duration in the two cases. It rests altogether in this, that the last involves a true organic entrance into the stream of the world's life, which the other does not.[62]

61. Ibid., 8
62. Ibid.

This is one of Nevin's chief concerns, which is voiced throughout many of his writings. Christ's work must be understood as having lasting value and worth on account of the incarnation. The hypostatic union must therefore be conceived as bringing the divine nature into vital union with humanity and thus remaining in force throughout human history.[63] As Nevin saw it, only as it rests on this foundation does Christ's death hold any real and lasting value to actually make an atonement that has any enduring efficacy to deal with the sin of the world. Anything less than this is a mere passing revelation which was here at one point in time, but is now gone. In this regard, Nevin claims complete support from the early Fathers of the Church:

> The ancient church fathers abound with this view, of the organic union of the divine life with the human in Christ; and through him in the Church, as lying at the foundation of all Christianity. Particularly is this the case with those, who occupy that most brilliant period in the history of the theology, which immediately followed the Sabellian and Arian heresies. Such men as Athanasius, the Gergories, and Basil, plant themselves continually on this high ground, as the only secure platform of the Christian faith and salvation. They insist clearly on the distinction between the show and the reality of an incarnation. To make Christ a mere theophany or avatar, involved, to their apprehension, the overthrow of the gospel. They felt too, and say over and over again, that the incarnation was of force,

63. On this, see particularly Nevin's articles in the *Mercersburg Review*, "Answer to Dorner" (600–602), and "Once for All."

for the race, and not simply for the single person
of Christ himself. They speak of him always, not
as the cause merely, but as the *principle* of the
new creation, which is represented accordingly
as flowing organically from his person, onward
to the last resurrection.[64]

Nevin then cites Isaak Dorner as an authority to support his understanding of the Fathers. But he shows too
that he himself was very much familiar with their thought,
and that he had been drinking deeply from their writings
for some time.[65] In a footnote, for example, he states that
"For one who has come to take any inward interest in the
subject, it is indeed refreshing to commune with the deep
Christological ideas of this old patristic divinity. Better *such*
mysticism, a thousand times, than the barren abstractions,
which have taken the place of it, in much at least of what is
called popular theology at the present day."[66]

After this, Nevin addresses Hodge's charge that he is a
Eutychian because of his contention that Christ's divine and
human natures form one life. Here he helpfully clarifies that

64. Nevin, *Antichrist*, 9.

65. This is also evidenced in many of his articles published
throughout the years following this controversy in the *Mercersburg
Review*, such as his four articles on the *Apostles' Creed* (1849), his three
articles on *Early Christianity* (1851–52), and his four articles on *Cyprian*
(1852). On Nevin's love for the early Church Fathers, Nichols states that
"he made himself at home with Irenaeus, Athanasius, Basil, and the
two Gregories. With some justification Dorner called Nevin Eastern
Orthodox in his orientation" (*Romanticism in American Theology*, 159).
With regard to parallels between Mercersburg and Eastern Orthodoxy,
see W. Bradford Littlejohn's excellent treatment in *The Mercersburg
Theology and the Quest for Reformed Catholicity*, 124–46.

66. Nevin, *Antichrist*, 10.

in his mind the term *life* is more closely related to the term *person* than to *nature*:

> Dr. Hodge charges me with Eutychianism, because I affirm the divine and human natures to have become so united in Christ, as to constitute one undivided life. The proof, as he gives it, is short; one life, he tells us, is only another word for one nature or φυσις, under which term Eutyches taught such a union of the two sides of our Savior's person as in fact reduced his humanity to a mere show; whence I am made to teach the same thing, or at least something no better. Words here, as we all know, are of most precarious force. I can only say that for me, *life* is not the same thing with nature, in the hypostatical mystery. I use the term rather to express, what I conceive to be involved in the idea of personality.[67]

Nevin goes even further than a mere defense of his own opinion here, however. While shielding himself against the charge of Eutychianism, he hurls the charge of Nestorianism back at Hodge, claiming that for Hodge the two natures of Christ, though professedly residing in one person, are mechanically thrown together. As Nevin interprets him, Hodge's doctrine of the incarnation implies that human nature is not brought into a real hypostatic union with the divine nature: "But what is personality, if it be capable of this broad dualism? . . . In what sense can the union of the two natures be *hypostatical*, if both are not brought to meet and rest in a strictly common centre?"[68] He continues

67. Ibid., 10.
68. Ibid., 10–11.

in this vein by asserting that the entire Princeton theology is but a mental abstraction thrown together in mechanical fashion to suit the dictates of human reasoning.

Nevin concludes then that the entirety of Charles Hodge's theological system is characterized by a general "Nestorianizing tendency." It is worthwhile to quote his indictment in this regard at length:

> [Hodge's] general theology carries a decidedly Nestorianizing aspect throughout. This is shown particularly in what might be termed the bald abstraction, in which all doctrinal ideas are made to stand. The Trinity is taken as a logical formula, rather than a living revelation of God through Jesus Christ. The relation of God to the world, is that of an artificer over against the mechanism of his own work. The last principle of things, is an outward decree, which it is his business to execute in a like outward way. Man is no organic whole . . . but a vast multitude of living units placed on the same theatre, by successive gen- erations, for moral trial. God imputes the sin of Adam to his posterity, not on the ground of any real unity of life between the parties, but purely of his own sovereign pleasure, just as he might have imputed the sin of fallen angels to men, if he had thought proper . . . They fell not so in the actual reality of life, but only in God's purpose and plan. Parallel with this mechanism of the curse, runs the mechanism also of redemption. The incarnation is an expedient, *contrived* to solve the problem of the atonement, and must be carefully held aloof from the whole process of the world's history under any other view, lest

it should lose this 'ex machina' character. Why it should have been delayed four thousand years, or why its action since should have been suspended on the common laws of our life in such a way as to move at so slow a rate over the face of the globe, is not clear; such however has been the divine will. After all, no absolutely new order of life has been introduced into the world by the occasion . . . The person of Christ itself, as such, forms not the specific revelation of the gospel, but simply his word and work as instrumentally disclosed through his agency. Divinity and humanity were indeed united in his life, but not in such a way as to be conjointly concerned at all in the same process of birth, growth, affection, work, suffering, and death. The humanity moreover, in this case, stood in no organic relation to our human life generally; it was simply the theophanic form, in which it was thought good that the Word should at this time appear. The second Adam, thus constituted, was made our representative again, like the first, by pure covenant and decree, and not on the ground at all of any inward qualification he had, by the constitution of his person, to become a new organic root for the race. He was in truth no such root whatever, but the outward author simply of a redemption, which is made over to his people in a foreign way.[69]

Thus we see again John Nevin's utter disdain for any theory concerning Christ and his work which implies any hint of an abstraction of Christ from humanity. He sums up his real feelings concerning the theological system of

69. Ibid., 11–12.

Charles Hodge thus: "In view of the whole, I can only say: If *this* be Calvinistic orthodoxy, my soul, come not thou into its secret, and unto its assembly, mine honor, be not thou united."[70]

CONCLUDING REMARKS

We have seen that John Williamson Nevin's theological system was centered on his understanding of the incarnation. By entering into human history in the person of Jesus Christ, the divine Logos came into organic union with humanity. This fact was, for Nevin, the foundation of man's redemption. Take this away, or relegate it to a mere mechanism by which Christ as an isolated individual could become the representative of a group of people by divine decree, and there is no real hope of redemption.

Charles Hodge criticized Nevin's theology on a number of levels. He claimed that it was one with the theological system of Friedrich Schleiermacher and consequently also that it was a vast departure from the faith of the Reformed Church in particular as well as the universal Church in general, and charged him along the way with a wide variety of heresies. The most fundamental problem Hodge had with Nevin's theology was his elevation of the incarnation over the death of Christ and the forensic imputation of Christ's righteousness to believers as the basis of man's redemption.

Nevin defended himself against Hodge's criticisms by clarifying that he was not slavishly following the theology of Schleiermacher, but was in fact more indebted to the

70. Ibid., 13.

early Church Fathers for his understanding of the hypostatic union than he was to any nineteenth century German theologian. In this way Nevin defended his orthodoxy and claimed that it was he who was in line with the historic creedal definitions of the person of Christ, not Hodge. Thus, to Hodge's accusation of Eutychianism, Nevin countered with the charge of Nestorianism and the assertion that Hodge was advocating a purely abstract Christology that was contrary to an orthodox understanding of redemption.

The relation these issues bear to the controversy between the two theologians on the nature of the Eucharist may by now be apparent. For Hodge, redemption was primarily a matter of legal declaration. Atonement and imputation, while rooted in the work of Christ in history, are applied to the believer by way of divine pronouncement, rather than by an actual communication of Christ's life through the mystical union. Thus, the sacraments must be held as subordinate to that declaration, and therefore only possess an edifying and sanctifying efficacy as the Spirit wills to use them to build up the faith of individual believers, who come into union with Christ quite apart from them. Nevin held, on the other hand, that while it remained true that God declares sinners righteous through faith and on account of Christ's work, this work itself derives its value and efficacy on the basis of who Christ *is*. From there, he argued that redemption is applied to Christians through a real, living, mystical union with the person of the incarnate Redeemer. Thus, salvation for Nevin ultimately flows from Christ's person to believers through a mystical union wrought by the Holy Spirit. This conditioned the central role which the sacramental ministry of the Church occupied in Nevin's system, as the preaching of the word and the administration of the sacraments were considered by him to be the means by which Christ's life is communicated to his people.

Hodge voiced some valid criticisms of Nevin. For instance, Nevin did seem to go farther than the Reformers or the Reformed Confessions did in making the incarnation, and not the cross, the basis of man's redemption. But even amidst his valid criticisms, Hodge dramatically overstated his case in claiming that Nevin was out of line with the entire universal Church in his doctrine of the incarnation. Nevin in fact had ample patristic support for his conception of the hypostatic union and its implications for man's redemption. Especially wide of the mark in this regard were Hodge's charges of Sabellianism and Eutychianism. Hodge was not as well acquainted with the relevant patristic writings on the hypostatic union as Nevin was. Consequently, he interpreted Nevin not as a theologian deeply indebted to the Fathers of the early church, but rather as little more than an expositor of the innovative, heterodox opinions of Friedrich Schleiermacher.

Hodge also over-reached in claiming that Nevin had no place for the atonement or imputation in his theological system. Here again he betrayed a tendency to view Nevin as nothing other than Schleiermacher *redivivus*. Nevin's continued clarifications about his relation to Schleiermacher should have guarded him against this accusation. Further, Nevin repeatedly called attention to the fact that he was trying to establish the efficacy of the atonement and the imputation of Christ's righteousness by emphasizing what he saw as most foundational—the incarnation of Christ and the vital union of believers with the incarnate, risen Savior.

Had Hodge taken Nevin's qualifications in this regard seriously, he still would have had considerable reservations about Nevin's theological system. However, he may have been a bit more congenial towards his former student than what is communicated in some of his more extremely stated accusations.

On the other hand, while Nevin's harsh response to the condescending tone of Hodge's review is understandable, his counter-accusation of Nestorianism does not paint a completely accurate picture of Hodge's Christology. Hodge, it is true, did have a tendency to speak of the person of Christ in a way that might lend itself to this charge (such as, for instance, when he insists that there is a *dualism* in Christ). However, Hodge's articulation of the incarnation, judged charitably, is able to claim essential fidelity to at least the broad guidelines set down in the definition of Chalcedon.[71]

Thus, the Christological aspects of Princeton-Mercersburg controversy were of utmost importance in setting the terms and tone of the overall debate between Hodge and Nevin. Yet, there sat behind the differences

71. For example, in *Systematic Theology, vol. 2*, Hodge would explain that "The union of the two natures in Christ is a personal or hypostatic union. By this is meant, in the first place, that it is not a mere indwelling of the divine nature analogous to the indwelling of the Spirit of God in his people. Much less is it a mere moral or sympathetic union; or a temporary and mutable relation between the two. In the second place, it is intended to affirm that the union is such that Christ is but one person" (390). And later Hodge argues that Nestorius, "obviously carried the distinction of natures too far, for neither he nor his followers could bring themselves to use the Scriptural language, "The Church of God which he purchased with his blood" (402).

between them on all these points even deeper divergences as to their underlying philosophical presuppositions and their respective understandings of the task of theology. Therefore, in order to rightly understand the theological conflict between Hodge and Nevin, we must consider more fully the impact their philosophical principles and theological methods had on the particular contours of the controversy. Accordingly, then, we shall revisit in the final chapter the same topic with which we began—the diverging theological systems of Princeton and Mercersburg.

4

Retrospective Reflections—
Princeton and Mercersburg Revisited

THE SYSTEMS OF HODGE AND NEVIN

OVER A decade after John Nevin penned his final response to Charles Hodge's review of *The Mystical Presence*, Hodge wrote an article in the *Princeton Review* entitled "What is Christianity." In that article Hodge reiterated and expanded upon many of the objections he had voiced against Nevin's theological system in 1848. He got at the heart of the matter between him and Nevin when he criticized Nevin's understanding of Christianity as follows: "the whole scheme of salvation is made to depend on a certain view of anthropology. Unless we believe in a generic humanity as an objective reality, a substance underlying all individual lives, we cannot believe the gospel."[1]

Hodge's assessment here was correct. Nevin's soteriological scheme, centered as it was on the union of God with generic humanity in Christ's person, was certainly dependent upon a realist anthropology. However, what Hodge did not seem to consider was the impact that nominalist

1. Hodge, "What is Christianity," 141.

categories had on his own thinking about the nature of the Christian gospel. Whereas Nevin hung his hat on the principle that mankind shares one undivided life which fell in Adam, Hodge's theory of redemption is dependent upon anthropological principles which led him to understand mankind as being little more than a collection of individual persons. Because of this conception of the nature of humanity, Hodge came to see the principle of legal representation as being the touchstone of Protestant orthodoxy. He therefore claims in the second volume of his *Systematic Theology* that Nevin's anthropological realism obliterates "the Church doctrine of the substitution of Christ."[2]

Consequently, given his philosophical commitments to nominalism and the principles of Scottish Common Sense realism, the only valid understanding of humanity for Hodge was that which can be ratified by the senses. Humanity is nothing more than the collection of all individual human persons, because this is what mankind is observed by the senses to be.[3] This good American dedica-

2. Hodge, *Systematic Theology, vol. 2*, 534–35. William DiPuccio's summary of the philosophical differences at work here is helpful: "Briefly stated, the underlying matter is whether the ideas of 'person' and 'life,' especially as they related to Christ, are to be regarded as simply an aggregate of individual qualities (nominalism) or a hypostatic reality (realism). If the former, then these ideas are essentially abstractions—conventional terms used to classify a family of like properties. If the latter, then 'person' and 'life' are ontological realities out of which these individual properties and attributes flow" (*The Interior Sense of Scripture*, 59).

3. William Evans has commented on the impact this had on Hodge's ecclesiology: "Thus, in the final analysis, the true church for Hodge is simply the 'aggregate' of individuals that have believed on Christ" (*Imputation and Impartation*, 368).

tion to the principles of Common Sense put Hodge at odds with all nineteenth century thinkers who were influenced by German philosophy (of which there were a very select few laboring on American soil), John Nevin no less than anyone else. Hodge himself had anticipated that this would be the case when studying in Berlin early in his career. Commenting on a theological discussion that had taken place among a group of German students one evening, at which he was present, Hodge wrote that, "This gave me occasion to remark the effect on their minds, of the universal attention to philosophy required of the students in Germany. They were acute and discriminating, but amazingly deficient in plain, healthy good sense."[4]

We can see Hodge's nominalist anthropology and representative principle played out rather clearly in his understanding of redemption: the mass of individual men are in sin because their first representative sinned, and this first sin was imputed to all subsequent human beings by divine decree. The corruption and death of all individual men is thus the penalty handed down as the divine punishment for the disobedience of the first man. In order to redeem these fallen men, therefore, Christ became a man so that he could win the victory over their curse by doing what Adam could not do as man's representative. He was fully obedient to God and endured to the point of death, taking the wrath of God upon himself for the forgiveness of the sins of his people. Consequently, also, Christ's righteousness is

---

4. Recorded in A. A. Hodge, *The Life of Charles Hodge*, 172. I was originally pointed to this quote by Mark Noll's introduction to Charles Hodge, *The Way of Life*, 15.

forensically imputed to all individual men for whom he was the representative.

As we noted earlier in chapter one, a characteristic feature throughout this understanding of redemption is the supremacy of the particular over the universal.[5] Any talk of an objective existence of universal humanity which may be distinguished from particular human persons was sheer nonsense to Hodge. And he was so confident that his representative principle was the only correct way to understand the plan of salvation that he would claim that it is "the simple and universally accepted view of the doctrine as held by all Protestants at the Reformation, and by them regarded as the corner-stone of the Gospel."[6]

But this federalist Princeton articulation of redemption, reliant as it was on nominalist and Common Sense principles, was to Nevin completely unacceptable. William DiPuccio has rightly said that, "Mercersburg regarded this error as the root of radical individualism and sectarianism which would destroy the unity of both the church and American society."[7] In contrast to that of Hodge, Nevin's

5. The comments of DiPuccio are again helpful on this point: "Hodge's theology of imputation, then, begins with Adam and Christ in their individuality. Subsequently, they are made to assume a representative role by divine fiat. As a result, the individual is said to be prior to the general or universal life of the race. A similar pattern is evident in Hodge's view of the church. The individual believer comes before the life of the church" (*The Interior Sense of Scripture*, 145).

6. *Systematic Theology, vol. 3*, 145.

7. DiPuccio, *The Interior Sense of Scripture*, 17. Nevin would claim concerning the philosophy of empiricism and Common Sense: "The whole tendency of this philosophy is towards materialism and infidelity; as we may see exemplified by its past history in other parts of the world, particularly in France. It may be associated, it is true,

metaphysic was conditioned by the notion that particular things are under-girded by objective universals. A proper understanding of humanity therefore mandates that it be conceived not simply as a collection of individual persons, but as an organic whole. According to Nevin, then, all individual human beings share one common life, the corruption of which must first be dealt with at its most foundational and universal level before it can be made to pass over into individual persons. For Hodge this made no sense, because to him, as an empiricist of the Common Sense school, what is real is only that which can be located and observed. Consequently, he claimed that "when it is said that the act of Adam was truly the act of the race, because he was a generic man, or that humanity as a general life acted in him,

---

with an opposite system; as commonly in this country, where it claims the spiritual and supernatural, indeed, as peculiarly its own province. But so far as such connection goes, it is outward only and traditional, not inward and real. The philosophy itself has no power to reach the spiritual and supernatural, and in pretending to do so, only drags it, in fact, downward into its own sphere, so that it is in the end truly neither one nor the other. It reasons from time to eternity with vast dexterity and ease, establishing, by strict Baconian comparison and induction, the existence of God, the immortality of the soul, and the truth of revelation; but it is all in such a way as turns eternity itself into time, and forces the whole invisible world to become a mere abstraction from the world of sense. The empirical understanding affects to become transcendent, (as Kant calls it,) and may please itself with having grasped in this way the truth which lies beyond its own horizon; but it is the illusion of one who dreams to be awake, and, behold, he is asleep: the object grasped, when all is done, belongs to the sphere of sense, and not to the sphere of spirit. This philosophy makes no room at all for *ideas* in the proper sense of the term; its ideas are all intellectual abstractions merely, that as such carry in themselves no necessary or universal force" (*Human Freedom and a Plea for Philosophy: Two Essays*, 43–44).

the words have no meaning. They convey no idea. As Dr. Nevin would say, they are an empty sound."[8] Thus, it may be concluded that Charles Hodge simply did not think in categories that allowed him to properly grasp Nevin's theology as a whole.

While for Hodge the representative principle was the foundation for all theology, Nevin considered the entire theory on which such a conception of redemption rests to be fundamentally shallow and abstract. According to him, Hodge's way of conceiving and articulating the redemption of man necessarily distorts the very nature of Christianity, as the federalism of Princeton sets up an isolated, abstract Christ who bears no real or living connection to the world he came to redeem. This for Nevin cuts the legs out from under Christian redemption, as it turns salvation into a matter of arbitrary divine decree, rather than a "real transaction of God in the world." He therefore states concerning all articulations of redemption that would presume to downplay the mediated presence of God in the world through the incarnation of Christ and the sacramental ministry of the Church:

> The only redemption it requires comes at last merely to this, that the parties that have been separated by sin should be brought together in form or fancy, without being reconciled in fact. The relation in which Christ stands to the whole object may be considered important and necessary, but it is altogether outward and mechanical, and no good reason appears why he should be a human Christ at all. He is the occasion by which men are brought near to God, not the real medium of this approach itself.[9]

8. Hodge, *What is Christianity*, 137–38.
9. Nevin, *Antichrist*, 38.

In contrast to such opinions, Nevin considered the hypostatic union of God with human nature in the person of Christ to be "the key, the only key, that unlocks the hidden mystery of the world. Turn this into a Gnostic phantasm, or Nestorian abstraction, and all theology becomes to the same extent uncertain and unreal."[10]

Hodge did not go quite as far as to turn the incarnation into a "Gnostic phantasm," of course. He could often speak in rather glowing terms about the incarnation and union with Christ. So, for instance,

> The Scriptures teach that the Logos is everlasting life, having life in Himself, and the source of life, physical, intellectual, and spiritual. They further teach that his incarnation was the necessary condition of the communication of spiritual life to the children of men. He, therefore, is the only Saviour, the only source of life to us. We become partakers of this life, by union with Him; this union is partly federal established in the councils of eternity; partly vital by the indwelling of the Holy Spirit; and partly voluntary and conscious by faith. It is to those who believe, to those who receive Him as God manifest in the flesh, that He becomes eternal life. For it is not they who live, but Christ who lives in them.[11]

But for a realist such as John Williamson Nevin, such statements—as long as they were couched within a system that held no conviction in humanity as having one life and confessed no vital union between God and this generic

10. Ibid., 53.

11. Hodge, *Systematic Theology, vol. 2,* 396–97.

humanity in the person of Christ—were not sufficient to guard one against the charge of "Nestorian abstraction."

The differences between the two men were also conditioned by what they considered to be the great dangers of their age. Their concerns in these areas, coupled with their divergent philosophical presuppositions, led them toward different understandings and uses of terms like "objective," "subjective," and "abstract."

One of Hodge's primary theological concerns (perhaps his *highest* theological concern) was to shield the Church against the nineteenth century influx of mystical subjectivism—most notably that of Friedrich Schleiermacher and the German theologians who followed him. He perceived this mystical and subjective theology to be one of the greatest threats against Reformed orthodoxy in his day. In his effort to guard against this mysticism, Hodge opted for the supremacy of objective propositions and an understanding of the Christian faith which held it to be above all else a system of doctrines: "In the Church . . . Christianity has always been a system of doctrine. Those who believe these doctrines are Christians; those who reject them, are, in the judgment of the Church, infidels and heretics."[12] This conception of Christianity as a system of doctrines led Hodge to view Nevin's continual assertions that Christianity is primarily a *life* as nothing but gross subjectivity. He would therefore declare concerning the Mercersburg Theology that, "That system, as developed in the writings of Dr. Nevin, and in the Mercersburg Review, is anti-Protestant in its theory of Christianity or the nature of religion; in its theory of the

12. Hodge, *Systematic Theology, vol. 1,* 179.

Church, of the relative authority of Scripture and tradition, of justification, of the sacraments, and of the ministry."[13]

Nevin, on the other hand, was constantly on guard against rationalism and theological abstraction. What Hodge claimed to be objective truth, Nevin often viewed as little more than empty mental constructs devoid of objective reality in the world. As Nevin saw it, for something to be "objective" it must possess a force that is existent and present in the world *here and now*. This led him to emphasize above all else the entrance of God into the stream of human life through the incarnation. The incarnation for Nevin gives everything Jesus did on earth an enduring force and ongoing effect in the world through his union with humanity in general and with the Church in particular.

It was this concern to safeguard the enduring force and power of the person and work of Christ in the world through the ministry of the Church which brought Nevin to oppose all purely forensic conceptions of redemption. While he believed the atonement wrought by Christ's death to be of vast importance—even going so far at times as to confess that it is "the ground of our redemption"[14]—his conception of the atonement was firmly rooted in his realist understanding of the incarnation. The atonement remains of enduring force in the world because of Christ's organic union with humanity, and it is applied to believers through a real, mystical union between their persons and the crucified, resurrected person of the Redeemer himself, as he is offered to them as a present reality through the Church's ministry of Word and Sacrament. Nevin considered any-

13. Hodge, "Dr. Schaff's Apostolic Church," 153.
14. Nevin, "Once for All," 100.

thing less than this to be barren abstraction. According to him, strictly forensic models of redemption tend to isolate Christ from the Church and the world, and, as he put it, "such isolation, alas, turns the atonement in fact into an abstraction, and robs it of all its living power."[15]

However (and this is a point at which Hodge profoundly misunderstood him), Nevin was very clear on numerous occasions that he was not positing a Christ who is found only within the believing subject. He held firmly to the orthodox Protestant tradition regarding the historical Christ, who is *extra nos*, but with whom we are made one through faith. Hence, in opposition to the subjectivism of the German mediating theologians, Nevin would contend that, "the authority of Christ's presence and person (objective Christianity exhibited to us in Christ) is the ground of all subjective Christianity. Faith, in its last and deepest sense, is simply submission . . . to such objective authority. The Gospel to which it bows is primarily an external Gospel."[16]

OVERALL ASSESSMENT OF THE CONTROVERSY

We have seen these fundamental differences between the two theological schools of Princeton and Mercersburg play out in the Eucharistic controversy between Hodge and Nevin in a number of ways. Their diverging theological tendencies led the two theologians to articulate, in the midst of this conflict, dramatically different conceptions of the nature of the Church and the Sacraments, the nature of history, the person of Christ, and the nature of redemption.

15. Ibid., 106
16. Nevin, "Answer to Dorner," 643.

Due to his philosophical and theological commitments to empiricism, Common Sense, and the dualist tendency of his thought, Hodge could not conceive of any true union between the earthly elements of the sacraments and the heavenly realities they signify. The Eucharist for him is efficacious by divine decree—in whomever the Spirit wills to work—but holds no objective grace due to the real Spirit-wrought presence of Jesus Christ in both his divine and human natures. Nevin, on the other hand, contended emphatically that the sacramental elements must possess a true union with the realities they signify. And he safeguarded his place in the Reformed tradition by emphasizing three essential features of historic Reformed sacramentology in particular: 1. a rejection of the idea of a *local* presence, 2. the necessity of faith in order for an actual reception of the present reality, and 3. the operation of the Holy Spirit to join the reality to the signs and to communicate Christ to the faithful. Nevin further held—following Calvin—that the Eucharist possesses an objective grace (namely, Christ himself) that is held out and offered to all, but only received by faith.

The divergent understandings which Hodge and Nevin had of the nature of the sacraments led them to mean different things by the sacramental terminology they employed throughout the controversy. For instance, when Hodge used the term *spiritual* with reference to Christ's presence in the Eucharist, he meant that there is only a presence of Christ's Spirit in the Sacrament. Christ therefore, according to Hodge, is present in the Eucharist in his divinity, but not in his full humanity as well. The dualistic conception of the person of Christ and his presence in the Eucharist necessitated by such a theory was unthinkable to Nevin, for in his mind Christ is and remains always the Incarnate One, whose divine and human natures are inseparably united. Without a real (albeit non-local) presence of the incarnate Christ in the Sacrament, there is no hope—no gospel in reality—for the communicant to grasp. Nevin held such a theory of the Sacrament to be fundamentally rationalist and subjective. Against Charles Hodge, then, John Nevin contended that the presence of Christ in the Eucharist is an objective presence of the *whole* Christ, in his divininity and humanity, and not merely a presence to the mind of the individual.

Consequently, in the Christological realm, Hodge's dualist theological tendency led him to view Nevin as fundamentally Eutychian in orientation because of his emphasis on the *union* of Christ's two natures. And in contrast, Nevin's organic bent led him to view Hodge as a Nestorian because of his emphasis on the *distinction* of Christ's two natures.

The two theologians also interpreted history in dramatically different ways. In this regard they were entirely consistent with their undelying philosophical commitments. Hodge tended to view historical data as a collection of facts to be arranged and systematized in service to propositional truth.[17] And Nevin, on the other hand, conceived of history as a living organism of sorts, into which the historian must in a sense enter in order to properly understand it.

---

17. According to Mark Noll, one of the main features of the Princeton theological method was its tendency to "regard theological truth in static categories which were not influenced by historical development" (*The Princeton Theology*, 30).

In his quest to arrive at the original and authentic Reformed doctrine of the Eucharist, then, Hodge saw all the relevent historical documents as being of similar weight. He therefore tended to abstract them from their historical context, thus considering the three Eucharistic theories he noticed within the Reformed churches of the sixteenth century to all be for the most part independent from each other. Nevin, on the other hand, was commited to an overtly organic theory of historical development. This commitment led him to seek to discern the connection which various historical ideas, movements, and documents bore to each other, as well as to the movement of history as a whole. Nevin was also keenly aware of the significance of historical context in determining how the various terms in use during bygone ages are to be understood. Rather than locating three independent views in the Reformed churches of the sixteenth century, Nevin discerned two complementary tendencies, which reached an ultimate climax and synthesis in the mind of Calvin and the authoritative Reformed Confessions of the late 1550s and early 1560s. While Nevin's theory of historical development could at times lead him into fanciful conclusions,[18] in this particular debate it served him well.

The most fundamental theological differences between Princeton and Mercersburg, however, were in the areas of Christology and soteriology. Hodge viewed Jesus Christ primarily as the representative of a group of individual men who became a man in order to pay the penalty for their sins

---

18. Such as in his Hegelian interpretation of the history of heresy as the organic development of the spirit of Antichrist in the world, which forms the basis for his argument in *Antichrist*.

and so that his righteousness might be imputed to them. Nevin did not deny these facts *per se*, but contended that in themselves they are not enough to reach man by way of a true redemption. For Nevin, the fundamental problem of the race is the corruption of sin rooted deep within human nature in its universal conception. Christ needed therefore to become man (not just *a man*) in order to raise humanity out of this corruption in his very person, thereby inaugurating within humanity itself—due to the hypostatic union— the principle of the New Creation.

According to Nevin, therefore, the essence of the Gospel was contained in the living reality of Jesus Christ himself. The incarnate Christ *is* redemption by virtue of who he is in the constitution of his own person: "All begins with the incarnation. The whole Gospel is enunciated in that overwhelming declaration, 'The Word became flesh.'"[19] The Christian is saved from sin and death as she/he is mystically united with the incarnate Christ by the Spirit and through the ministry of the Church. The Church and the Sacraments are central here in that the Church is the sphere in which Christ promises to be present to save, and the sacraments are the means by which the life of Christ is communicated to the faithful.

But Nevin's theory of redemption, according to Charles Hodge, tended to do away with all hope of assurance for the believer. As Hodge saw it, emphasizing the incarnation and mystical union with Christ while taking the focus off the atonement and the imputation of Christ's alien righteousness to individuals served only to transfer all hope from that which is *extra nos* to that which is merely *intra nos*. Hodge

19. Nevin, *Antichrist*, 19.

accordingly declared concerning Nevin's understanding of the Gospel that,

> This system . . . sends the sinner naked and shiv-
> ering into the presence of God, with nothing to
> rely upon but the modicum of theanthropic life
> that flickers in his own bosom. He has no righ-
> teousness but what is inherent . . . If he feels him-
> self to be wretched, and miserable, and poor, and
> blind, he is so, and there is no help for him. All his
> treasures are within himself. If his theanthropic
> life does not make him righteous, and holy, and
> blessed, there is nothing else can do it.[20]

Yet here we are reminded once again of Hodge's tendency to equate Nevin's theology with that of Schleiermacher.
To Hodge, it mattered little how much Nevin qualified that
he was seeking only to establish and safeguard the doctrines of atonement and imputation. Nor did it help things
when Nevin claimed, as he frequently did, that he rejected
those elements in Schleiermacher's thought which ran him
into heterodox extremes. Hodge considered such clarifications to be little more than empty words, for, as he saw it,
Nevin presumed to strike at the very life-spot of Protestant
orthodoxy—the principle of federal representation and the
forensic imputation of Christ's alien righteousness to believers. And conversely, Nevin interpreted Hodge as offering
nothing more than an isolated, abstract Christ who had no
power to save *in reality*. To Hodge's federalism, therefore,
Nevin could only say, "If *this* be Calvinistic orthodoxy, my
soul, come not thou into its secret, and unto its assembly,
mine honor, be not thou united."[21]

20. Hodge, "What is Christianity," 159.
21. Nevin, *Antichrist*, 13.

Conclusion

CHARLES HODGE and John Williamson Nevin continually battled against different theological enemies throughout their careers. And while they were allies on some fronts (such as in their mutual rejection or Charles Finney's "New Measures" revivalism), they nevertheless considered each other adversaries in many of the theological wars they waged. Although the occasion for the most notable public controversy between Hodge and Nevin was a debate over the doctrine of the Reformed Church on the Lord's Supper, the theological contours of that conflict demonstrate that the real issue between the systems of Princeton and Mercersburg had to do with fundamental philosophical and theological presuppositions which transcended their respective positions on any one particular point of doctrine.

Charles Hodge won the day in the hearts and minds of American Reformed Christians. He is considered by many to be the father of modern American Presbyterian orthodoxy. John Williamson Nevin, on the other hand, while garnering interest within academic circles from time to time, has not enjoyed nearly the same theological legacy as his Princeton antagonist. Whereas there still exist today many institutions which pride themselves on carrying on the Princeton tradition that Charles Hodge so staunchly defended, there are few institutions which claim the theology of Mercersburg for their heritage. The great American born theologian John Williamson Nevin, it seems, was just not American enough for his ideas to have gained a fair hearing in a country so enamored with the ideals of common sense. And on top of being too German, Nevin's theology was too historically oriented, too sacramental, and in general too "churchly" to have had much hope for survival in "the land of the free."

Not surprisingly, the drastic differences that separated these two great nineteenth century American theologians remained unresolved throughout their careers. As we have seen, the disparity between them was so fundamental and so vast that there was little hope that the chasm could be bridged. Recognizing this, B. A. Gerrish has perceptively observed: "Hodge was a predestinarian Calvinist, Nevin was a sacramental Calvinist, and their debate may make one wonder if it is possible to be both at once."[1]

Yet, Calvin himself was both at once. So for those who wish to hold on to their Calvinist heritage fully— both in terms of its doctrine of the divine decrees as well as Calvin's robust sacramental theology—the situation is not hopeless. From such a perspective, it might be held that both Hodge and Nevin erred equally in that they allowed one of these important elements of traditional Calvinist theology to drown out the other. And it also might be held, from such a perspective, that it is of utmost importance for Reformed Christians of the present day to listen attentively to the concerns of both Charles Hodge and John Nevin, so that we do not end up unwittingly covering over important elements of the very historic tradition to which we confess to ad-

1. Gerrish, *Grace and Gratitude*, 170.

here. From this standpoint, in fact, it might even be argued that the theological schools of Princeton and Mercersburg needed each other in the nineteenth century, and that they continue to need each other today.

If nothing else, the nineteenth century Eucharistic controversy between Charles Hodge and John Williamson Nevin demonstrates for us in the twenty-first century that debates on particular points of doctrine are very rarely as simple as they may seem to be on the surface. They are rather conditioned by differences which may be more fundamental than any of the participants realize at the time, and are consequently very seldom resolved without the interlocutors first fully understanding each other, in order that these fundamental issues may be adequately addressed. Due to the theological commitments necessitated by their divergent philosophical presuppositions and theological methods, Hodge and Nevin were in large measure hindered from truly grasping and appreciating the significant concerns raised by each other in the midst of the controversy. This episode of American religious history should serve as a caution to all of us who are involved in theological study to be aware of the presuppositions and commitments which condition our own thinking, and to attempt to discern them in others, so that we might be able to understand both ourselves and those with whom we differ rightly. In this way, we might actually make significant progress toward fulfilling that great apostolic ideal—"speaking the truth in love."

Bibliography

Adger, John. "Calvin Defended Against Drs. Cunningham and Hodge." *The Southern Presbyterian Review*, vol. 27, 1876, 133–66.

Ahlstrom, Sydney. *A Religious History of the American People*. New Haven: Yale University, 2004.

———. "The Scottish Philosophy and American Theology." *Church History*, vol. 24, 1955, 257–72.

Anderson, Robert W. *A Bicentennial Remembrance: Charles Hodge; a Look at the Life and Witness of the Great Princeton. Theologian*. Charolette, NC: Fundamental Presbyterian, 1997

Appel, Theodore. *The Life and Work of John Williamson Nevin*. New York: Arno, 1961.

Brenner, Scott Francis. "Nevin and the Mercersburg Theology." *Theology Today*, vol. 12, 1955, 43–56.

Calhoun, David B. *Princeton Seminary, vol. 1: Faith and Learning, 1812-1868*. Edinburgh: Banner of Truth, 1994.

———. *Princeton Seminary, vol. 2: The Majestic Testimony, 1869-1929*. Edinburgh: Banner of Truth, 1996.

Calvin, John. *Calvin's Commentaries*. Translated by John Pringle. Grand Rapids, MI: Baker, 1999. (Volumes VII, VIII, XVII, and XX.)

———. *The Institutes of the Christian Religion*. Edited by John T. McNeil. Translated by Ford Lewis Battles. Philadelphia: Westminster Press, 1960.

———. *Theological Treatises*. J.K.S. Reid Ed. Louisville: Westminster John Knox, 1954.

Carlough, William L. "German Idealism and the Theology of John W Nevin." *Reformed Review*. Vol.15, 1962, 37–45.

———. *A Historical Comparison of the Theology of John Williamson Nevin and Contemporary Protestant Sacramentalism*. Ann Arbor, MI: University Microfilms, 1961.

Crisp, Oliver D. "Federalism Vs Realism: Charles Hodge, Augustus Strong and William Shedd on the Imputation of Sin." *International Journal of Systematic Theology*. Vol. 8, 2006, 55–71.

Davis, Thomas J. *This is My Body: The Presence of Christ in Reformation Thought*. Grand Rapids: Baker Academic, 2008.

DeBie, Linden J. *Speculative Theology and Common-Sense Religion: Mercersburg and the Conservative Roots of American Religion*. Eugene, OR: Pickwick, 2008.

Dick, John. *Lectures on Theology, Volume II*. Philadelphia: Edward C. Biddle, 1837.

DiPuccio, William. *The Interior Sense of Scripture: The Sacred Hermeneutics of John Williamson Nevin*. Macon, GA: Mercer University, 1998.

Evans, William Borden. *Imputation and Impartation: Union with Christ in 19th Century American Reformed Theology*. PhD diss., Vanderbilt University, 1996.

Farley, Michael A. "The Liturgical Theology of John Williamson Nevin." *Studia Liturgica*. Vol. 33, 2003, 204–22.

Garcia, Mark A. *Life in Christ: Union with Christ and Twofold Grace in Calvin's Theology*. Colorado Springs: Paternoster, 2008.

Gerrish, B.A. *Grace and Gratitude: The Eucharistic Theology of John Calvin*. Edinburgh: T&T Clark, 1993.

———. "The Lord's Supper in the Reformed Confessions." *Theology Today*, 23 (July 1966): 224–43.

———. *A Prince of the Church: Schleiermacher and the Beginning of Modern Theology*. Philadelphia: Fortress, 1984.

———. *Tradition in the Modern World: Reformed Theology in the Nineteenth Century*. Chicago: University of Chicago, 1961.

Hamilton, Ian. "The Life and Works of Charles Hodge." *Knowing the Mind of God: Papers Read at the 2003 Westminster Conference*. Mirfield: Westminster Conference, 2004.

Hamstra, Sam Jr. and Arie J. Griffioen. (Editors) *Reformed Confessionalism in Nineteenth Century America: Essays on the Thought of John Williamson Nevin*. Lanham, MD: Scarecrow, 1995.

Hart, Darryl G. "Divided Between Heart and Mind: The Critical Period for Protestant Thought in America." *Journal of Ecclesiastical History*. Vol. 38, 1987, 254–70.

———. *John Williamson Nevin: High Church Calvinist*. Phillipsburg, NJ: Presbyterian and Reformed, 2005.

Hatch, Nathan. *The Democratization of American Christianity*. New Haven: Yale University, 1989.

Hewett, Glenn Alden. *Regeneration and Morality: A Study of Charles Finney, Charles Hodge, John W, Nevin, and Horace Bushnell*. Brooklyn, NY: Carlson, 1991.

Hicks Peter. *The Philosophy of Charles Hodge: A 19th Century Evangelical Approach to Reason, Knowledge, and Truth*. Edwin Mellen, 1997.

Hodge, A.A. *The Life of Charles Hodge*. New York: Charles Scribner's Sons, 1880.

Hodge, Charles. *The Church and its Polity*. New York: T. Nelson, 1879.

———. *Commentary on Ephesians*. Edinburgh: Banner of Truth, 1991.

———. *Commentary on Romans*. London: Banner of Truth, 1972.

———. *Commentary on 1 and 2 Corinthians*. Edinburgh: Banner of Truth, 1974.

———. *Conference Papers or Analyses of Discourses, Doctrinal and Practical*. New York: Charles Scribner's Sons, 1879.

———. "Doctrine of the Reformed Church on the Lord's Supper." *The Biblical Repertory and Princeton Review*. Vol. XX, 1848, 227–78.

———. "Dr. Schaff's Apostolic Church." *The Biblical Repertory and Princeton Review*. Vol. XXVI, 1854, 148–92.

———. *Essays and Reviews*. New York: R. Carter, 1857.

———. "The First and the Second Adam." *The Biblical Repertory and Princeton Review*. Vol. XXXII, 1860, 335–76.

———. "Idea of the Church." *The Biblical Repertory and Princeton Review*. Vol. XXV, 1853, 249–90.

———. *Justification by Faith Alone*. Hobbs, N.M.: Trinity Foundation, 1995.

———. "Nature of Man." *The Biblical Repertory and Princeton Review*. Vol. XXXVII, 1865, 111–35.

———. *Princeton Sermons: Outlines of Discourses, Doctrinal and Practical*. London: Banner of Truth, 1958.

———. *Princeton Versus the New Divinity: The Meaning of Sin, Grace, Salvation, Revival*. Edinburgh: Banner of Truth, 2001.

———. "Schaff's Protestantism." *The Biblical Repertory and Princeton Review.* Vol. XVII, 1845, 625–36.

———. *Systematic Theology: Volume I, Theology.* Peabody, MA: Hendrickson, 2001.

———. *Systematic Theology: Volume II, Anthropology.* Peabody, MA: Hendrickson, 2001.

———. *Systematic Theology: Volume III, Soteriology.* Peabody, MA: Hendrickson, 2001.

———. "Truth, Charity, and Unity." *The Biblical Repertory and Princeton Review.* Vol. XL, 1868, 169–92.

———. *The Way of Life.* Edited by Mark Noll. New York: Paulist Press, 1987.

———. "What is Christianity?" *The Biblical Repertory and Princeton Review.* Vol. XXXII, 1860, 118–61.

Hoffecker, Andrew W. *Piety and the Princeton Theologians.* Phillipsburg, NJ: Presbyterian and Reformed, 1981.

Holifield, E. Brooks. "Mercersburg, Princeton, and the South : The Sacramental Controversy in the Nineteenth Century." *Journal of Presbyterian History.* Vol. 54, 1976, p 238–57.

———. *Theology in America.* New Haven: Yale University, 2003.

Horne, Mark. *Real Union or Legal Fiction? John Williamson Nevin's Controversy with Charles Hodge Over the Imputation of Adam's Sin.* Online: http://www.hornes.org/theologia/content/mark_horne/real_union_or_legal_fiction.htm#39a, 1997.

Horton, Michael S. *People and Place: A Covenant Ecclesiology.* Louisville: Westminster John Knox, 2008.

Littlejohn, W. Bradford. *The Mercersburg Theology and the Quest for Reformed Catholicity.* Eugene, OR: Pickwick, 2009.

Maxwell, Jack Martin. *Worship and Reformed Theology: The Liturgical Lessons of Mercersburg.* Pittsburg: Pickwick, 1976.

Mathison, Keith. *Given for You: Reclaiming Calvin's Doctrine of the Lord's Supper.* Phillipsburg, NJ: P&R, 2002.

Muller, Richard. "Calvin and the Calvinists: Assessing Continuities and Discontinuities between the Reformation and Orthodoxy, Part I." *Calvin Theological Journal*, vol. 30, 1995, 345–75.

————. "Calvin and the Calvinists: Assessing Continuities and Discontinuities between the Reformation and Orthodoxy, Part II." *Calvin Theological Journal*, vol. 31, 1996, 125–60.

Nevin, John Williamson. "Answer to Professor Dorner". *Mercersburg Review*. Vol. XV, 1868, 534–646.

————. "The Anti-Creed Heresy." *Mercersburg Review*. Vol. IV, 1852, 606–20.

————. *Anxious Bench, AntiChrist, and the Sermon on Catholic Unity*. Edited by Augustine Thompson. Eugene, OR: Wipf and Stock, 2000.

————. "The Apostles' Creed" (3 articles). *Mercersburg Review*. Vol. I, 1849. Article I: *Outward History of the Creed*, 105–27. Article II: *Its Inward Constitution and Form*, 201–21. Article III: *Its Material Structure and Organism*, 313–47.

————. "Bible Anthropology." *Mercersburg Review*. Vol. XXIV, 1877, 330–65.

————. "Catholicism." *Mercersburg Review*. Vol. III, 1851, 1–26.

————. *Catholic and Reformed: Selected Theological Writings of John Williamson Nevin*. Edited by Charles Yrigoyen Jr. and George H. Bricker. Pittsburgh, PA: Pickwick Press, 1978.

————. "Cyprian" (4 articles). *Mercersburg Review*. Vol. IV, 1852. Article I: 259–277. Article II: 335–387. Article III: 417–52. Article IV: 513–63.

————. "Doctrine of the Reformed Church on the Lord's Supper." *Mercersburg Review*. Vol. II, 1850, 421–548.

————. *Dr. Nevin's Theology: Based on Manuscript Classrom Lectures*. Compiled and Edited by William H. Erb. Reading, PA: I.M. Beaver, 1913.

————. *The History and Genius of the Heidelberg Catechism*. Chambersburg, PA: The German Reformed Church, 1847.

————. "Hodge on the Ephesians" (2 articles). *Mercersburg Review*. Vol. IX, 1857. Article I: 46–83. Article II: 192–245.

————. *Human Freedom and a Plea for Philosophy: Two Essays*. Mercersburg, PA, 1850.

————. *The Mystical Presence and other Writings on the Eucharist*. Edited by Bard Thompson and George H. Bricker. Boston: United Church Press, 1966.

————. *The Mystical Presence: A Vindication of the Reformed or Calvinistic Doctrine of the Holy Eucharist.* Edited by Augustine Thompson. Eugene, OR: Wipf and Stock, 2000.

————. "Nature and Grace." *Mercersburg Review.* Vol. XIX, 1872, 485–509.

————. "The New Creation in Christ." *Mercersburg Review.* Vol. II, 1850, 1–11.

————. "Noel on Baptism." *Mercersburg Review.* Vol. II, 1850, 231–65.

————. "Once for All." *Mercersburg Review.* Vol. XVII, 1870, 100–124.

————. "Puritanism and the Creed." *Mercersburg Review.* Vol. I, 1849, 585–603.

————. *The Reformed Pastor: Lectures on Pastoral Theology.* Edited by Sam Hamstra Jr. Eugene, OR: Pickwick, 2006.

————. "The Revelation of God in Christ." *Mercersburg Review.* Vol. XVIII, 1871, 325–42.

————. "Thoughts on the Church" (2 articles). *Mercersburg Review.* Vol. X, 1858. Article I: 169–98. Article II: 383–425.

————. "Wilberforce on the Eucharist." *Mercersburg Review.* Vol. VI, 1854, 161–87.

————. "Wilberforce on the Incarnation." *Mercersburg Review.* Vol. II, 1850, 164–96.

Nichols, James Hastings. *The Mercersburg Theology.* New York: Oxford Uniiversity, 1966.

————. *Romanticism in American Theology: Nevin and Schaff at Mercersburg.* University of Chicago, 1961.

Noll, Mark. *America's God: From Jonathan Edwards to Abraham Lincoln.* New York: Oxford University, 2002.

————. "The Princeton Review." *Westminster Theological Journal.* Vol. 50, 1988, 283–304.

————. *The Princeton Theology.* Grand rapids: Baker, 2001.

Pelikan, Jaroslav. *The Christian Tradition, Volume 5: Christian Doctrine in Modern Culture.* Chicago: University of Chicago, 1989.

Richards, George Warren. "The Mercersburg Theology: Its Purpose and Principles. *Church History.* Vol. 20, 1951, 42–55.

Rorem, Paul. "The Consensus Tigurinus: Did Calvin Compromise?" *Calvinus Sacrae Scripturae Professor.* Ed. by Wilhelm H. Neusner. Grand Rapids: Eerdman's, 1994, 72–90.

Sandeen, Ernest R. "The Princeton Theology: One Source of Biblical Literalism in American Protestantism." *Church History*. Vol. 31, 1962, 307–21.

Schaff, Philip. Schaff, Philip. *The Principle of Protestantism*. Edited by Bard Thompson and George Bricker. Eugene, OR: Wipf and Stock, 2004.

———. *Reformed and Catholic: Selected Historical and Theological Writings of Philip Schaff*. Edited by Charles Yrigoyen Jr. and George M. Bricker. Pittsburgh: Pickwick, 1979.

Schleiermacher, Friedrich. *The Christian Faith*. Two Volumes. Edited by H.R. Mackintosh and J.S. Stewart. New York: Harper and Row, 1963.

Shriver, George H. "Passages in Friendship: John W. Nevin to Charles Hodge." *Journal of Presbyterian History*. Vol. 58, 1980, 116–22.

Spear, Wayne R. "Calvin and Westminster on the Lord's Supper: Exegetical and Theological Considerations." *The Westminster Confession into the 21st Century, Volume 3*. Edited by J. Ligon Duncan. Fearn, Ross-Shire: Mentor, 2009, 385–414.

Stewart, John W., and James H. Morehead. (Editors) *Charles Hodge Revisited: A Critical Appraisal of his Life and Work*. Grand Rapids: Eerdmans, 2002.

Thorp, Willard (Editor). *The Lives of Eighteen from Princeton*. Princeton, NJ: Princeton University, 1946.

Wallace, Peter J. "History and Sacrament: John Williamson Nevin and Charles Hodge on the Lord's Supper." *Mid-America Journal of Theology*. Vol. 11, 2000, 171–201.

Wells, David. *Reformed Theology in America: A History of its Modern Development*. Grand Rapids: Baker, 1997.

Welch, Claude. *Protestant Thought in the Nineteenth Century: Volume, 1799-1870*. New Haven: Yale University, 1972.

Wentz, Richard E. *John Williamson Nevin: American Theologian*. Oxford University, 1997.

Willis, David. "A Reformed Doctrine of the Eucharist and Ministry and its Implications for Roman Catholic Dialogues." *Journal of Ecumenical Studies*. Vol. 21, 1984, 295–309.

www.ingramcontent.com/pod-product-compliance
Lightning Source LLC
Chambersburg PA
CBHW060308100426
42812CB00003B/702